RESTRAINTS ON WAR

RESTRAINTS ON WAR

Studies in the Limitation of Armed Conflict

Edited by

MICHAEL HOWARD

OXFORD UNIVERSITY PRESS

1979

Oxford University Press, Walton Street, Oxford OX2 6DP

OXFORD LONDON GLASGOW
NEW YORK TORONTO MELBOURNE WELLINGTON
IBADAN NAIROBI DAR ES SALAAM LUSAKA CAPE TOWN
KUALA LUMPUR SINGAPORE JAKARTA HONG KONG TOKYO
DELHI BOMBAY CALCUTTA MADRAS KARACHI

ISBN O 19 822545 8

© *Oxford University Press 1979.*

Typeset by CCC and printed and bound at William Clowes & Sons Limited, Beccles and London.

EDITOR'S PREFACE

The enclosed studies are based on a lecture course delivered in the University of Oxford in the Spring of 1977. They were made possible by a grant from the Cyril Foster Fund of the University and the Editor wishes to record his gratitude to the Chairman and Board of Management of the Fund.

All Souls College,   MICHAEL HOWARD
Oxford

CONTENTS

TEMPERAMENTA BELLI:
CAN WAR BE CONTROLLED?

Michael Howard

The assumption is very generally made that control and restraint are alien to the very nature of war. Clausewitz opened his *On War* with a statement to this effect. 'War' he wrote, 'is an act of force to compel our enemy to do our will . . . Attached to force are certain self-imposed, imperceptible limitations hardly worth mentioning, known as international law and custom, but they scarcely weaken it . . . To introduce the principle of moderation into the theory of war itself would always lead to logical absurdity.'[1]

Much depends on the meaning one attaches to such terms as 'limitation', 'control', 'restraint', and 'moderation'. But the proposition that war is in its essence 'uncontrollable' is an untenable one, as Clausewitz himself recognized elsewhere in his text.[2] War, at least as the term has been understood in western societies since the Middle Ages, is not the condition of generalized and random violence pictured by Thomas Hobbes as 'the state of nature'. It is on the contrary a highly social activity – an activity indeed which demands from the groups which engage in it a unique intensity of societal organization and control. It involves the reciprocal use of organized force between two or more social groups, directed according to an overall plan or series of plans for the achievement of a political object. Rousseau was surely right when he stated, in contradiction to Hobbes, that war without social organization is inconceivable; that it is only as a member of a state, or comparable social organism, that man makes war.[3] Indeed the requirement for social control imposed by the necessities of war has normally been a major element, if not *the* major element, in the development of state structures.

All this predicates a distinction between 'war' on the one hand and riot, piracy, brigandage, generalized insurrection and random violence on the other. The wars of which we speak consist of the purposive and instrumental use of force by legitimized authorities. It is a discrete condition with a certain coherent and orderly predictability of its own. Members of belligerent armed forces normally operate according to orders transmitted through a highly-structured hierarchy. They may legitimately kill members of opposing armed forces in battle unless the latter explicitly surrender, and there is a distinct risk that they will kill them even then. The persons and property of civilians in zones of military operations or within reach of military projectiles are at risk even if they are totally non-combatant. In areas occupied by military forces engaged in combat civilians are subject to the legal authority of those forces, whether they be friendly or hostile. Enemy nationals in a country at war are likely to be put under severe constraints. None of this may be agreeable, but it is all highly *predictable*, and comes about as the result of conscious decision by effective authorities.

The state of war indeed involves at every level of government and society the imposition of authoritative control. Governments, in so far as they are able, will control the production, allocation, and utilization of resources, including human resources. Individual freedom of movement, of expression, of communication and of consumption will be controlled in 'the national interest'. The military authorities will use the resources at their disposal to achieve an objective according to a planned strategy implemented through a coherent and authoritative hierarchy which possesses exceptional sanctions for the enforcement of obedience. One still occasionally comes across the old-fashioned liberal stereotype of the soldier as a stupid and brutal *Untermensch* dedicated to random violence. Such characters can indeed be found in most armies, but equally most armies go to great lengths to discipline and if possible eliminate them. In reality the military, at least in 'advanced' countries, constitute highly motivated, well-organized and cohesive groups, educated, technologically sophisticated, with a professional obsession with order, discipline, and channels of command. Even in the least developed societies they are likely to exhibit these traits to a greater degree than the rest of the population.[4]

The prime characteristic of the military is not that they use violence, nor even that they use violence legitimized by virtue of their function as instruments of the state. It is that they use that violence with great *deliberation*. Such violence, purposeful, deliberate, and legitimized is normally known as *force*, and the use of force between states is what we mean by war. War consists of such deliberate, controlled, and purposeful acts of force combined and harmonized to attain what are ultimately political objectives. That such acts may be horrifying in their consequences goes without saying. Their object is quite precisely the infliction of destruction, suffering, and death, 'the trial of moral and physical forces', to quote Clausewitz again, 'through the medium of the latter'.[5] But strategy consists in determining how, where, and upon whom that destruction is to be inflicted. Such destruction can be random, as was German and British 'area' bombing in 1940–3, for lack of technical means to make it precise. It can also be random as the result of a deliberate decision, as when in seventeenth- and eighteenth-century warfare the territory of an opponent was ravaged, or in more recent conflicts hostages were shot or towns burned by occupation forces in retaliation for *franc tireur* activity; or, in the contemporary world, urban guerrillas detonate bombs in cities to demonstrate their ubiquity and effectiveness. Such decisions and the consequences which flow from them normally are the result of deliberate choice and explicit orders, and they require for their implementation, even in the case of guerrilla activities, a highly articulated structure of control. When random violence is the result of the breakdown of such control, as in the notorious My Lai massacre of Vietnamese civilians by U.S. forces in 1969, when troops lapse from disciplined and discriminating use of force into purposeless and indiscriminate violence, the result is as repugnant to military professionalism as it is to transcendent ethical values.*

Military activity thus carries an intrinsic imperative towards control; an imperative derived from the need to

---

* A distinction must be made in the case of siege-warfare, when cities were quite deliberately 'put to the sack', involving indiscriminate massacre, looting and rapine, if they refused summonses to surrender *en règle*.

maintain order and discipline, to conserve both moral and material forces and ensure that these are always responsive to direction. These military criteria however will not necessarily coincide with the dictates of humanity. For example, the military case against area bombing would be, not that it was inhumane, but that it was ineffective in achieving its objective of demoralizing the civilian population and reducing war production; that it was psychologically 'counter-productive' and materially wasteful.†[6] General William T. Sherman's very comparable strategy in 1864 however, no less ferociously indiscriminate in the destruction it inflicted on the Confederacy, could by the same criteria be adjudged a military success: it did effectively reduce the civil population of the Confederacy to a state of near-despair. The military principle of 'economy of force' may sometimes conveniently coincide with the dictates of transcendent moral values, but there is little historical justification for assuming that this will always be the case.

To control and limit the conduct of war is thus not inherently impossible; indeed without controls and limitations war cannot be conducted at all. The difficulty lies in introducing and maintaining controls and limits derived from criteria other than those inherent in sound strategy and the requirement for 'good order and military discipline'. Such criteria can normally be grouped under two heads. There are the categorical imperatives derived from the general value-systems of the culture concerned; and there are the prudential considerations which demand that, to put it at its lowest, the costs of war do not in the long run outweigh its benefits.

The first of these criteria dominated thinking about war during the era of ecclesiastical dominance which lasted in Europe until the sixteenth century, as clerical apologists, attempting to accommodate the necessities of warfare to the ethical imperatives of the Christian religion, refined the concept of 'the just war'. The second became dominant from the seventeenth to the nineteenth centuries, the age of Grotius;

---

† Against this, its protagonists reasonably argue that it threw the German Air Force on to the defensive and enabled Allied air forces to gain command of the air over the battlefields in 1942-5.

when it was assumed, in the words of Montesquieu, that 'the law of nations is naturally founded on this principle, that different nations ought in time of peace to do one another all the good they can, and in time of war as little injury as possible without prejudicing their real interests.'[7] This second approach concentrated on what was and was not permissible in wars between states without concerning itself about the rights and wrongs of any particular war. The first, without ignoring this question of *jus in bello*, was primarily concerned with *jus ad bellum* – the justice or injustice of the cause for which one fought. And this concern was to reappear in a yet stronger form in the wars of 'national self-determination' or 'national liberation' of the nineteenth and twentieth centuries.

During this period, war in western societies passed, broadly speaking, through three phases.[8] From about the eleventh century war ceased to be the struggle for physical survival it had been during the 'barbarian' invasions and became gradually a ritualized conflict within a warrior culture, partly agonistic, partly juristic. Wars were agonistic in so far as they were extensions of competitive games and tournaments, juristic in so far as they were an appeal to a 'higher tribunal' where no legal remedy was available. In both capacities highly formalized 'rules of war' were appropriate and indeed necessary. But in general the restraints observed in warfare within Christendom did not apply in the 'just wars' which Christians fought to defend, to purify, or to extend their faith. To submit to restraints which prejudiced ones chances of victory when fighting in a righteous cause, to accept the concept of *jus in bello* when one had an unquestionable *jus ad bellum*, was a paradox which few warring communities, then or since, found it easy to accept.

The 'Grotian' period, during which jurists explicitly abjured any interest in the cause of a conflict and concerned themselves only with its conduct, stretched approximately from the Peace of Westphalia in 1648 to the Hague Conferences on the eve of the First World War, and was the golden age of the *jus in bello*, of formal, positive constraints on the conduct of war. But such behaviour postulated a very stable structure of society and a highly homogeneous culture shared to an equal degree by all its members. It required on the part of governments an overriding concern for the maintenance of social and political stability, and a capacity to maintain that stability within their own domestic systems. Since war was always an instrument of state policy, as Clausewitz discerned, it would be 'limited' in so far as that policy was limited; but once a state decided to pursue a policy of revolution and conquest and was no longer prepared to be bound by established norms, it would fight 'absolute' and unconstrained war. No restraints would be imposed other than those arising out of the nature of war itself.[9]

Such, unfortunately, was the way in which warfare has developed in the third of our periods, the twentieth century, when the concept of 'the just war' has re-emerged with renewed vehemence; whether in the assertion of national identities, or of ideological absolutes, or a combination of the two. Such conflicts of their nature tend to be 'zero-sum games' in which each side considers itself to be fighting for the preservation of all its cultural values, for its very survival, against an alien and irreconcilable adversary. Nor are such perceptions necessarily false. In the Second World War Hitler attacked both Poland and the Soviet Union with the intention of destroying their societies and reconstructing them as German colonies.[10] As an outcome of that war both German and Japanese cultural values were completely transformed by their victorious enemies. So, as an outcome of the thirty-years' war in South-East Asia, have been the cultural values of the societies of Cambodia and Vietnam. There is little reason to expect anything different as the result of a comparable conflict in Southern Africa. Wars today can be irreversible in their consequences. There is thus little inclination to conduct them with restraint.

A strong case can indeed be made for the argument that if war *can* be limited, if the belligerents can be reasonable enough to accept extraneous limitations on its conduct and regard the enemy almost as a *frère adversaire*, they should be reasonable enough to avoid fighting altogether. This sentiment became widespread towards the end of the eighteenth century: a reaction against the formal and artificial constraints of

European warfare which simply provided a life-style for a parasitic warrior-aristocracy, a growing feeling that one should not fight at all except in extreme situations, and then do so with no holds barred. This was the view that Tolstoy put into the mouth of Prince Andrei on the eve of the Battle of Borodino in *War and Peace*:[11]

We have been playing at war – that's what's vile! We play at magnanimity and all the rest of it . . . if there was none of this magnanimity business in warfare, we should never go to war, except for something worth facing certain death for, as now . . . War is not a polite recreation but the vilest thing in life, and we ought to understand that and not play at war. Our attitude towards the fearful necessity of war ought to be stern and serious. It boils down to this: we should have done with humbug and let war be war and not a game.

Agreed limitations on warfare imply rational understandings with an enemy who, if he can be reasoned with, should not be an enemy. 'Laws of war', *jus in bello*, do imply a rather sophisticated warrior culture in which adversaries are conscious of an overriding common interest in preserving the rules of the game; and it may be precisely this kind of aristocratic society that a war is being fought to destroy.

In any case, two developments over the past hundred years have combined to introduce into wars, at least between industrialized states, an increasing element of *totality*. The first of these has been the development of mass democracy, the erosion of those aristocratic élites whose kinship, cultural if not actual, across national boundaries had strengthened the kind of constraints to which Andrei objected and whose chivalric concepts of honour could occasionally be found mitigating the ruthlessness of the First and even the Second World War.[12] The growth of mass societies and the possibility of government control of communications made total alienation between belligerent societies, their mutual perceptions as figures of total evil, all too easy. The fundamental tragedy of the First World War was that what was to a very large extent an old-style 'war of policy' to readjust the balance of power in Europe, another War of Austrian Succession, became seen, because of mass participation and mass propaganda, as a total war between incompatible and mutually exclusive cultures, when in fact it need have been nothing of the kind.

Linked with this development in society has been the simultaneous development in technology which created new modes of destruction of an indiscriminate kind: the submarine at sea, which could not possibly operate within the old restrictions of Prize Law and, more significant still, air power in its earlier and cruder manifestations. Finally with the advent of thermonuclear weapons total war threatens total destruction on a scale incompatible with any criterion either of political calculation or of military necessity. For the first time the Clausewitzian analysis is put in question: nuclear war, if it came, could be total, not because of the political objectives of the belligerents, but because of the military tools at their disposal. Western strategists plan for the mass destruction of Soviet cities, and vice versa, not because their political masters have any serious political motive for extirpating the societies of their adversaries, but because in a grotesque inversion of logic the means now dictate the ends. Both on moral and on prudential grounds therefore it has seemed increasingly clear, as the twentieth century has pursued its course, that war should not simply be limited; it should be abolished, outlawed.

This was something new. The existence of war was until the nineteenth century accepted as inevitable by everyone except a few Christian sects. The problem was to determine the limitations upon its conduct. Aquinas and others in the Middle Ages had defined the nature of a 'just war': a war waged by a legitimate authority, for a cause in itself just, to make reparation for an injury or to restore what had been wrongly seized, and with the intention of advancing good and avoiding evil. To this sixteenth-century jurists like Suarez and Vitoria added prudential considerations. There should be a reasonable prospect of victory. Every attempt should have been made to reconcile the differences by peaceful means. No direct attack should be made against non-combatants. The amount of force used should not be disproportionate to the end to be achieved.[13] By the time of Grotius more prudential considerations began, as we have seen, to predominate. By the eighteenth century the concept of the 'just war' had disappeared. 'War waged in its right form must be regarded as just on both sides' stated the great Swiss jurist Eméric Vattel. This was the heyday of 'limited war'; and as the technical developments of the nineteenth century widened the destructive scope of warfare and made such limits seem ever more difficult to maintain, new conventions had to be drawn up (The Declaration of Paris of 1856, the Geneva Convention of 1864, the Declaration of Brussels of 1874, the Hague Conventions of 1899 and 1907) in an attempt to rescue and reassert them.

Even during this era of 'limited wars', however, a significant cleavage persisted between the attitude of continental and of British jurists. From the eighteenth century onwards continental jurists accepted the distinction made by Rousseau, that war is a conflict not between individuals but between *states*, and assumed that individuals took part in it only in so far as they voluntarily abandoned their private status and, by taking up arms, became the agents of the state. This meant that not only the lives and the property of private individuals, so far as possible, should be protected from belligerent acts, but their economic activities as well; which effectively meant their trade. This doctrine, of course, long antedated Rousseau. Its great protagonist was Hugo Grotius himself,[14] and its most stubborn champions were the Dutch; whose capacity to carry on their struggle for independence in the sixteenth and seventeenth centuries depended entirely on their freedom to trade, including freedom to trade with their enemies. But for the British during the same period blockade of commerce became a major weapon of war; blockade which, however narrowly defined, inflicted inevitable and deliberate hardship upon enemy civilians. So from John Selden onwards[15] British jurists argued that the economic activities of civilians, in so far as they made possible the belligerent acts of governments, were a perfectly legitimate target for military activity. The British in fact looked beyond the immediate conflict of armed forces to the war-fighting capabilities of the states which sustained them, and took a consistently hard line, as Bryan Ranft shows in his chapter, over such matters as the definition of contraband, the rights of neutrals, and the right of search.[16]

It was to be the British doctrine that prevailed. As the

nineteenth century progressed, virtually every economic, intellectual, and political development in Europe eroded the distinction between 'society' and 'state'. Even if private individuals did not become formal 'agents of the state' through compulsory military service, the extension of political and emotional participation in national affairs left ever fewer areas of pure 'privacy'. Nineteenth-century conflicts such as the American Civil War and the Franco-Prussian War gave a foretaste of the lesson of the First World War: that no military victories, however spectacular, were likely to be decisive so long as civil society retained the will and the capacity to carry on the war. Paradoxically, at the time when the Geneva and the Hague Conventions were mitigating the horrors of the battlefield, as Professor Best describes in his chapter, to the extent almost of giving the military a privileged status, the scope of armed conflict was being inexorably extended far beyond that battlefield. The lessons of the First World War were summed up in a paper which the British Naval Staff presented in 1921 to the Committee of Imperial Defence:[17] 'Nothing can be clearer than the fact that modern war resolves itself into an attempt to throttle the national life. Waged by the whole power of the nation, its ultimate object is to bring pressure on the mass of the enemy people, distressing them by every possible means, so as to compel the enemy's government to submit to terms.'

But if the objective of military effort was *not* the opposing armed forces but 'the mass of the enemy people', the most direct and economical way of deploying that effort was surely to strike directly at that mass, and air forces, particularly the Royal Air Force, justified their claims to institutional independence by their capacity to do just that. There was some talk of 'surgical strikes' against arms factories and centres of government, but a generation was to pass before technology made this practicable, and even those who advocated such strikes regarded the 'morale' of the enemy working population to be an entirely legitimate objective.[18] The vain attempts to control the genie of air power before it escaped from all control in the Second World War and inflicted such irreparable damage on the peoples and the cultural heritage of Europe and Japan, are described by Donald Watt in the body of this work.

It was very largely this growing destructiveness of war, the damage mutually inflicted by armed forces even before the advent of air power placed the whole social structure in hazard, that led governments to give support, after 1918, to the movement to 'outlaw' war itself and to create, not a *jus ad bellum*, but a *jus contra bellum*. In the Covenant of the League of Nations, in the Pact of Paris (the Kellogg–Briand Pact) of 1928, and in the United Nations Charter the initiation of war for any purpose was condemned. The signatories of the Kellogg–Briand Pact 'condemn[ed] recourse to war for the solution of international controversies and renounce[d] it as an instrument of national policy in their relations with one another.'[19] The creation by this Pact of a *jus contra bellum* was made one of the bases for the charges levelled against the defendants before the International Military Tribunal at Nuremberg in 1946 for 'crimes against peace', as the Hague and Geneva Conventions were made the basis of the charges of 'war crimes'. An entirely new category of law had to be created to encompass their 'crimes against humanity'.[20] It is interesting in this context to note that the United Nations Charter avoids reference to the term 'war' altogether. It refers only to 'acts of aggression', 'breaches of the peace' and 'threats to peace'; while all signatories, by Article 2 para. 4, pledged themselves to 'refrain in their international relations from the threat or use of force against the territorial integrity or political independence of any state'.[21]

Having abolished war, it might be considered paradoxical, not to say pessimistic, to continue to make regulations for controlling it. This thought clearly crossed the collective mind of the International Law Commission of the United Nations in 1949 when it came to consider the codification of the Laws of War. 'It was considered that, if the Commission, at the very beginning of its work, were to undertake this study, public opinion might interpret its action as showing lack of confidence in the efficiency of the means at the disposal of the United Nations for maintaining peace.'[22] But as Professor Hersch Lauterpacht drily observed, 'The phenomenon of war does not fully admit of treatment in accordance with the canons of logic. Banished as a legal institution, war now remains an *event*, calling for legal regulation for the sake of humanity and the dignity of man'.[23] So in 1949 a further Geneva Convention was signed, extending to civilians the rights which previous conventions had recognized as inhering in members of the armed forces with respect to humane treatment at the hands of belligerents.

About such further attempts since 1945 to refine and update legal restraints on war, *jus in bello*, we have space in this volume to consider only those in respect of maritime conflicts, at once the most complex and the most frequent. But perhaps of yet greater significance in the nuclear age have been the *prudential* attempts to impose restraints on conflict; attempts initiated not so much from humanitarian concern with the belligerents themselves, whether military or civilian, as out of the realization that technology has now given mankind the capacity quite literally to destroy itself. Little could be done to mitigate the totality of wars when that totality was caused by the deliberate policy of the belligerents. But if destructive-ness is the consequence not of the object aimed at but of the means employed, then military and moral restraints are not necessarily incompatible. The concept of 'limited war' between advanced industrial communities becomes not simply possible but necessary, if the use of force is to serve any political object; including that of defending one's own territory or that of one's allies. In their chapters John Garnett and Laurence Martin consider the practical implications and problems of such a concept. Such restraints can no longer be regarded as an intrusion from the moral into the military sphere. They belong to the category of those purely military constraints considered at the beginning of this chapter, in the absence of which war becomes mere indiscriminate and inconclusive violence.

During the quarter of a century which has passed since strategic analysts began to refine the concept of 'limited war', the world has mercifully been spared the experience of major conflicts between industrialized states. It has however wit-nessed widespread conflicts of a different kind; struggles subsumed under the title of 'wars of national liberation', usually fought by indigenous groups against European colonial authorities or, as in Southern Africa, régimes asserting a racial hegemony. These groups seldom had any status in international law: they were rebels against the jurisdiction of governments enjoying full state sovereignty. Nevertheless at the International Conference on Human Rights held at Tehran in 1968 a resolution was passed demanding that persons struggling against 'racist or colonial régimes' should be protected against 'inhuman or brutal treatment and treated as prisoners of war': that 'freedom fighters', in fact, should be afforded the protection of international law.[24] A further conference of experts was convened in Geneva to implement this resolution, which in 1977 agreed on the Convention which Gerald Draper describes in the final chapter of this work.

Such a demand of course goes to the root of the international system itself. There has been a long history concerning the award of belligerent status to insurgent forces in civil war. There has been, as Geoffrey Best shows us, an equally historic and acrimonious controversy over the rights and duties of civilians taking up arms against an invader. But the principle that only 'legitimate authorities', states and their agents, have the right to make war and to claim recognition and protection in war, has been the basis of the whole system of rational, controllable, inter-state conflict. Naturally such a system is biased in favour of the *status quo* and places independent, non-state actors at a considerable disadvantage. But it is easy to forget what an enormous advance was made in the direction of a just, peaceable and orderly society when the chaotic permissiveness of violence in fourteenth- and fifteenth-century Europe was codified and limited, over the centuries, into orderly relations between 'perfect states'. The problem is to extend the traditional system to encompass and humanize this new kind of conflict. But it can be done only if the objectives of both sides are moderate and compatible. No amount of legal draftsmanship can prevent a quest for total victory from leading to total war.

War, as we said at the beginning, involves inherent constraints. It is carried out by men making conscious choices and obedient to hierarchical commands. Orders can be given to spare as well as to destroy. Whatever the objective aimed at or the weapons used, the plea of military necessity has to be brought into focus with two other requirements, arising from the nature of man as a moral and as a social being. The first imposes an ethical rule: one does not cease to be a moral being when one takes up arms, even if required by military necessity to commit immoral acts. There are other tribunals to which one may be called to account. And the second imposes a prudential rule: one should not behave to one's adversary in such a way as to make subsequent reconciliation impossible. War is instrumental, not elemental: its only legitimate object is a better peace.

NOTES

1. Carl von Clausewitz, *On War* (Princeton, 1977), p. 75.
2. 'War is simply the continuation of political intercourse . . . war cannot be divorced from political life; and whenever this occurs in our thinking about war, the many links that connect the two elements are destroyed and we are left with something pointless and devoid of sense.' Clausewitz, op. cit., p. 605.
3. J.-J. Rousseau, *The State of War*. Reprinted in M. G. Forsyth *et al.* (eds.), *The Theory of International Relations* (London, 1970), p. 167.
4. See Stanislav Andreski, *Military Organization and Society* (London, 1954) and Gavin Kennedy, *The Military in the Third World* (London, 1974), *passim*.
5. Clausewitz, op. cit., p. 127.
6. See Noble Frankland, *The Bombing Offensive Against Germany : Outlines and Perspective* (London, 1965) for a balanced discussion.
7. Montesquieu, *The Spirit of the Laws* (New York, 1940), p. 5.
8. A similar but not identical tripartite division is to be found in Robert E. Osgood and Robert W. Tucker, *Force, Order and Justice* (Baltimore, Md., 1967). For an extended treatment see Michael Howard, *War in European History* (Oxford, 1976).
9. Clausewitz, op. cit., p. 606.
10. Norman Rich, *Hitler's War Aims: the Establishment of the New Order* (London, 1974).
11. Leo Tolstoy, *War and Peace* (Harmondsworth, 1957), p. 921.
12. For a radical attack on such constraints see Thorstein Veblen, *An Inquiry 'into the Nature of Peace* (New York, 2nd edn., 1919).

13. There is a brief and useful summary in Sydney D. Bailey, *Prohibitions and Restraints on War* (Oxford, 1972), pp. 1–16.
14. Hugo Grotius, *The Freedom of the Seas* (trans. J. B. Scott, New York, 1916).
15. John Selden, *Mare Clausum: the Right and Dominion of the Sea* (London, 1663).
16. See especially G. N. Clark, *The Dutch Alliance and the War Against French Trade* (Manchester, 1923).
17. CAB 16. 46/47. CID 131–c.
18. See Sir Charles Webster and Noble Frankland, *The Strategic Air Offensive Against Germany* (London, 1961. 4 vols.), vol. IV, Appendix 2.
19. Texts in James T. Shotwell, *War as an Instrument of National Policy and its Renunciation in the Peace of Paris* (New York, 1929), p. 302.
20. Bailey, op. cit., p. 158. Ian Brownlie, *International Law and the Use of Force by States* (Oxford, 1963), pp. 167–95.
21. H. G. Nicholas, *The United Nations as a Political Institution* (Oxford, 1967), p. 208.
22. Bailey, op. cit., p. 91.
23. Quoted in Lothar Kotsch, *The Concept of War in Contemporary History and International Law* (Geneva, 1956), p. 294.
24. Bailey, op. cit., p. 92.

2

RESTRAINTS ON WAR BY LAND
BEFORE 1945
Geoffrey Best

Two stories from the early years of this century exemplify
both the power of the idea of restraint on war and some of the
intrinsic difficulties of implementing it. The diplomat and
man of letters, Maurice Baring, when an officer in the Army
Flying Corps, found himself in Hazebrouck town square about
the middle of October 1914. A stationary lorry-load of
German prisoners of war was being booed and menaced by
the crowd. 'Someone began throwing things. I addressed the
crowd. "Le grand Napoléon a dit", I said, "qu'il n'y a rien de
plus lâche que de maltraiter les prisonniers". He may have
said so. I hope he did. In any case the effect on the crowd was
immediate . . .'[1] To remind a francophone mob of Napoleon
was to evoke a presence still supernaturally authoritative,
although by then nearly a century old. But it was not
necessary, when invoking authorities for restraint in war in
the early years of this century, to go so far back or beyond a
great man's grave. Not many months before, General Hugh
L. Scott, commanding the U.S. troops at Fort Bliss on the
Mexican border, sent across the border to the insurgent leader
Pancho Villa, the Fidel Castro of the day, a pamphlet copy of
'The Hague Rules': the code of restraints on war by land
which had been finally agreed on by the self-styled civilized
nations in 1907. 'He spent hours poring over it. It interested
and amused him hugely,' wrote John Reed. 'He said: "What
is this Hague Conference? Was there a representative of
Mexico there? . . . it seems to me a funny thing to make rules
about war. It is not a game. What is the difference between
civilised war and any other kind of war?"'[2]

Yet the idea of restraint in war was not just, with Pancho
Villa, the grim joke he thought it was. In those remarks, which
even if he cannot be proved to have made them seem to have
been just the sort of remarks he would have made, he was

doing himself less than justice. Like many others, who unreflectingly and instinctively reject the notion of limiting violence in war, Pancho Villa himself in fact did limit his, to an extent and in ways which made his style of guerrilla operations recognizably like those of, for example, the Chinese People's Army in the 30s and 40s, and the Algerian F.L.N. in the 1950s. He freed captured Government soldiers if they had been conscripted and could thus be presumed to be serving unwillingly. He severely disciplined his own men if they killed wantonly; he had some sort of a field hospital and he looked after politically acceptable wounded prisoners as well as the wounded of his own side. In the tale about Pancho Villa and the story told by Maurice Baring lie all the essentials of the history of this theme. General Scott and the Hague Rules, which were an appendix to one of the Hague Conventions of 1907, exemplify the written law, carried to its highest level in international treaties and conventions signed and ratified by the 'high contracting parties'; as states denominate themselves at such levels and on such occasions. 'Le grand Napoléon', a professional of professionals, exemplifies the respect for the customary law of civilized Europe which was all the law of war there was in his age, but which was none the less felt by military professionals and men of honour to have some binding force. Pancho Villa, though to the European (and U.S.A.) professional eye lawless and lamentable, exemplifies the customary restraints and prohibitions which have some-times marked the wars of relatively underdeveloped and undeveloped peoples. Our modern Law of War (or international humanitarian law, as it is increasingly known) is the confluence of these three tributary streams.

Although most of this chapter will be about modern times, justice cannot be done to the moral weight and historical depth of the theme unless it is well understood that the idea of restraint in war is no sentimental venture of more or less modern man but a still continuing preoccupation of humane and moral-minded people with a history as long as that of humanity itself.

Historians of the subject delight to show how a law of war was familiar to the ancient Greeks, and how much was made of it by the Romans. Medieval writers – theologians, jurists, canonists – wrote a good deal about the law of war, and some medieval fighters paid some attention to it. Shakespeare's play *Henry V* is rich in illustrations both of the idea of restraint and of the passions and prejudices militating against it; though in what proportions Shakespeare was representing later medieval or early modern practices and principles, or whether they were largely the same, I cannot say. Through the sixteenth and early seventeenth centuries, the idea of restraint in war came to seem only the more attractive on account of its tragic absence in the imperial aggressions, the religious wars, and the mere anarchies of those years. Now appeared the 'fountain-head' books of the founders of modern public international law: the Dominican Francisco Vitoria in Salamanca in the early sixteenth century; the Jesuit Francisco Suarez, professor at Coimbra in the later sixteenth century; the Italian Alberico Gentili, Regius Professor of Civil Law at Oxford from 1587; and best known of all, that international man Hugo Grotius, who was born at Delft in 1583 and died *en route* from Sweden to France in 1645. Upon the pioneer guidance of these great men, Grotius's successors through the later seventeenth and eighteenth centuries advanced to the compilation of quite comprehensive statements of the customary law of Christian Europe, governing the belligerent phases of international relations as well as the pacific.

Of course this 'international law' was only customary, and was still rather fluid, even experimental. All the time there were arguments about who had broken the law and whether they were justified in doing so. It was not the least of the many areas of customary morality of which Frederick the Great made fun when it suited him.[3] But it was more honoured, one can hardly fail to conclude, in the observance than the breach. The force of custom and conventional practice, especially when it was enforced by a transnational aristocratic ruling class, and when it was backed by the philanthropic inclinations of the age, was enormously strong. The Earl of Chatham made one of his most powerful speeches in criticism of the employment by the British commanders in North America of barbarous native auxiliaries.[4] Dr. Johnson poured his eloquence into a pamphlet pleading the cause of the French prisoners of war in England, whom the British Government seemed to be neglecting.[5] Commanders at the beginnings of campaigns would negotiate conventions (local and limited in duration) for the respect of each other's wounded and medical units, specifying the signs under which such units and their personnel should be protected. Prisoners became better treated, and might often be exchanged.[6] When the Committee of Public Safety in May 1794 superimposed a revolutionary ideology and civilian attitudes on the customary standards, and ordered French troops on the north-east frontier to refuse quarter to British and Hanoverian soldiers, those troops connived with their commanders to disobey the order. What is equally to be admired, the British Duke of York, commanding those British and Hanoverian soldiers, expressly ordered them not to refuse quarter by way of reprisal. Napoleon was quite a stickler for the observance of customary law so far as logistics and strategy permitted (which often meant not much), and seems to have been on quite good ground in his complaint that the British treatment of prisoners fell further below the highest accepted standards than the French.

Those wars, the Revolutionary and Napoleonic ones, certainly witnessed a great quantity of the horrors and disasters which it is the object of the law of war to avert; yet the idea of the law of war was never seriously disputed or rejected; and the century which followed proved to be, in fact, its golden age, with the 1860s as its golden decade. That was when the converging streams of international humanitarian opinion, international law (developing very fast through the second half of the nineteenth century) and military modernization produced the three great landmarks of our modern Law of War. In 1863, United States Army General Order No. 100, *Instructions for the Government of Armies of the United States in the Field*, provided the first example of a manual for the conduct of war on land comprehensively attentive to the current state of customary law and the standards which a self-respecting civilized state should set for itself. Also known as 'Lieber's Code' (after the excellent German-born jurist who was principally responsible for it), it became the basis for all subsequent discussion and formulation through the next fifty years. In 1864 the first Geneva Convention, designed for the protection of the sick and wounded in land war, marked the great step forward of an international agreement signed by 'high contracting parties' for their common restraint and welfare. Four years later, in 1868, the St. Petersburg Convention prohibited the use of certain types of missiles on the ground that belligerents were not unrestricted in their means of making war, and that therefore missiles of unnecessary nastiness could and should properly be outlawed.

From the 1860s to the First World War it was almost possible, perhaps, to measure the extent of the hold which the idea of restraint in war had on the public mind of Europe by the volume of clamour alleging the breaking or the neglect of it. This happy phase began with the Franco-Prussian War. The Prussians gave their opponents a propaganda opportunity they perhaps need not have given, and the French made the most of it. The world was soon more than adequately informed about German severity against French partisans and their civilian supporters; the *francs-tireurs* which then made such a stir in the world and continued to haunt the German military imagination through 1914. The world was also made fully aware of the German bombardments of Strasbourg, Peronne etc. and of course, climactically, Paris. These German excesses, if indeed they were such, which was arguable, were in areas of that customary law which by now was filling fat sections of the international law books. But when it came to breaches or neglects of the Geneva Convention, the first bit of international statute law, no one could doubt as to which of the two great powers was more at fault. The Germans took it seriously and observed it quite creditably. The French were doubly at fault, first, in not knowing much about it, and second, when they did wake up to its existence, by getting it wrong.[7] While French soldiers were likely to be taking pot-shots at German ambulance men conscientiously signalling their position by means of Red Cross flags, French civilians, hearing rumours of this miraculously effective symbol, in some places festooned their houses along the German lines of advance with Red

Crosses, imagining that they would thus gain immunity from billeting, requisitions, and so on. Nor was it only French civilians who got it wrong. The Red Cross message, more or less garbled, ran like wildfire round the humanitarian world. Staff officers on both sides were annoyed by the cool presumption of medical and sanitary do-gooders who turned up from all over and thought that by sporting a Red Cross arm-band and carrying a case of bandages they were entitled to wander around the battle zone at will. And it is difficult to say whether more offence was given to military propriety by the Irish Volunteer Ambulance which downed stretchers and helped to defend Châteaudun under the impression that this was an episode in the long battle between Rome and Wittenberg, or by the ghouls who combed the battlefield after the fighting was done, some of whom were found to be covering with the Red Cross emblem their hideous ancient business of killing off the wounded and robbing the dead.

The Geneva Convention and its governing idea thus came out of the Franco-Prussian war somewhat battered, and in Germany above all there was a great deal of indignation at the way the French had failed to understand and observe it, and the ways in which, as many Germans seemed to have felt, their conscientious observance of it under such circumstances had involved them in some disadvantages. But despite these mishaps, there was nothing here which could not be put right by improved legislation.[8] The Red Cross from now on was a force to be reckoned with. Between 1871 and the 1914–18 war there was a positive vogue for it as a mixed philanthropic and patriotic venture in which the highest-born could engage without loss of status and in which civilians could do something war-related without much risk, to an extent which made some think that the age of chivalry (Burke's, not Froissart's) had returned.

No more extraordinary instance of this could be found than an incident during the war between Serbia and Bulgaria in late 1885.[9] The Red Cross societies in each country sought supplies from the wealthier countries of Europe; those supplies were plentifully available and were routed towards them through Vienna. It was not difficult to transport them from

Vienna to Belgrade but to get them to Sofia was a different
question, the main lines from Vienna to Sofia running through
Serbia! The Austrian Red Cross society, however, sought from
King Milan of Serbia permission to send the supplies destined
for Bulgaria through his territory. Permission was granted
and the Red Cross materials were safely conducted to the
Bulgarian outposts. The explanation of this episode must be as
unusual as was the episode itself, because the Balkans were the
last place in Europe (except perhaps the Iberian peninsula) in
which, as a matter of historic fact, humanity in war was
commonly expected or found. The episode nevertheless
occurred and it fitted well with the mood of an epoch which
supported internationalism and the peace movement and took
pride in its spreading humanitarianism at the same time as its
militarists, nationalists, and imperialists were egging on the
first great arms race; an epoch which therefore not surprisingly
culminated in the conferences at the Hague in 1899 and 1907
called Conferences for Peace and Disarmament but clearly
more bent towards what Joseph Conrad, a curiously close
observer of those doings, called the 'solemnly official recognition of the Earth as a House of Strife'.[10] Much the same
judgement on the ambivalent character of the Hague
Conferences may be found in a remark made by a Japanese
diplomat to a European one at that time. The 1899 Hague
Conference was the first at which the Japanese were present
as international equals of the European and American powers
which had hitherto engrossed the making of international
law. But by what title had Japan got there? 'We show
ourselves at least your equals in scientific butchery, and at
once we are admitted to your council tables as civilized men.'[11]
The Japanese diplomat seems to have been a bit worried
about the moral character of the club his country had just
joined.

This survey is to go up to 1945, but the sketch of the
assembling of the laws of land war is now done. That
assemblage was virtually completed between 1899 and 1907.
Between then and the end of the Second World War, very
little more was added. To the Hague Convention and Rules of
those years, regarded as a code of combat law, nothing

subsequently was added except the 1925 Geneva protocol on
Gas Warfare. Indeed there was more movement in the Geneva
line of explicitly humanitarian law. The 1864 convention
which experience had shown to be unsatisfactory in several
important respects was replaced by a better one in 1906
(better, anyway, from the soldier's point of view) and by other
even better ones in 1929 when prisoners of war also became
recognized as primary subjects of Red Cross concern. Such
were the three levels of restraint at which the two world wars
were supposed to be fought: the international conventions
associated with the Hague and Geneva; the manuals of
military conduct in which each armed service embodied the
conventions and rules to which its Government had agreed,
but which of course went far beyond them in scope and detail;
and, what too often has been left out of account, the notions of
the members of those armed services themselves about
restraint, some of which worked for it and some of which
clearly did not.

What soldiers actually think about conduct in war, and
how their thoughts affect their conduct, is an area of this
subject which has so far been very little explored. The legal
and official literature, understandably enough, takes no notice
of the possibility that within armed forces a kind of sub-culture
or 'private' culture may exist, the norms and tendencies of
which may conflict with those prescribed in the manuals of
military conduct, etc. Certain it is, that armies have their own
inner lives and cultures, concerned largely of course with the
violence which is their professional business. Equally certain
must it be that such cultures largely determine the modes in
which violence is used, following the categories of what that
culture considers fair, unfair, manly, courageous, cowardly,
and so on.

The question then for the historian who wishes to embrace
all relevant possibilities is: what are the relations between this
private military culture which will lay its persuasive claims
upon the thinking and behaviour of at least the regular soldier
who has been acclimatized to it, and the public political
culture from which his army as a whole ostensibly derives its
standards and instructions? To put it in another way: how

much is left of the law of land war as it issues from the mind of Professor Thomas Erskine Holland of All Souls College, Oxford, by the time it has filtered down to his contemporaries, private soldiers Ortheris, Learoyd, and Mulvaney? Very much may be left when an army is as well-disciplined as, for example, the German army normally was; but few armies are so well-disciplined as that. There seems in this area of military thought and conduct to be an unknown factor which needs to be much more fully examined than it yet has been.

   Three examples will have to suffice. First, the taking of prisoners. It has long been central to our law of war that quarter should be given and prisoners decently cared for, under a regime of specific rights and obligations. The International Red Cross did not begin with a concern about prisoners of war, but very early in its history it came to recognize in them a category of suffering soldiers just as needy as the sick and wounded, and most of its celebrity in both World Wars derived from its activities on prisoners' behalf. Now it seems probable that some parts of popular military culture may clash awkwardly with the public law concerning prisoners. All kinds of rumours spread like wildfire among troops and behind the lines, often including grim stories about what the enemy does to those who surrender or try to do so; which inevitably have the effect of stimulating a thirst for reprisals. Such stories about the refusal of quarter sometimes have something in them. One has read and heard often enough of bodies of troops or individuals among them with whom it has been a point of pride not to give quarter; and this within even the most law-minded armies, serving the apparently most civilized states.

   Second, loot. Loot, pillage, plunder etc. gradually came under the ban of the law of land war for a variety of reasons, prominent among them the fact that soldiers in pursuit of loot inevitably broke discipline and did damage, the effects of which could rebound upon their own army and its future prospects. Yet there is plentiful evidence from all wars that soldiers in all but the most extraordinarily disciplined and law-observing armies have looted whenever opportunity has offered and have considered the pursuit of loot a kind of soldier's natural right. Third, women. Ideas about women and sex obviously have always taken a large place in a culture which is as wholly male a culture as one could hope to find. There is no need to elaborate upon this. But the implications for the observance of the laws of war are serious. Women have not yet much appeared as armed combatants, but have usually been the larger part of that non-combatant world to which both the law of war and ordinary military discipline ostensibly offer protection. Here, however, comes another clash between the requirements of the law and the probable expectations of the common soldier. A free hand with the girls seems always to have been a basic component of what the common soldier hopes for, believes he deserves, and feels entitled, when circumstances permit, to get; forcibly, if nothing else will get it. The literature of war is full of evidence of this disagreeable dark edge to military behaviour and no more need be said about it here than that, according to a speaker in the House of Lords in a recent debate, this sort of thing is still with us. *The Times* of 5 November 1976 duly reported the Earl of Mansfield saying in a debate upon the Sexual Offences (Amendment) Bill: 'Juries today were wider [nowadays] in their sympathies with the woman than they were in the past. When I practised, I never lost a case of rape when I was defending because juries in the past were more predominantly male. If one got on the right note one could always invite them to conclude that either they got up to that sort of thing when they were servicemen or they would have, had they had the courage.'[12]

That excursus through just three of the many areas of soldiers' behaviour, where officially prescribed restraints may conflict with the cultural norms of at any rate regular soldiers, is offered merely to indicate one of the many obscurer causes why those restraints tend to be less than perfectly observed. The remainder of this chapter will examine the more obvious, accessible, and documented parts of the subject, inquiring particularly into the less successful aspects of the story and their explanation. That impressive structure of international law which became built into and around the Geneva and Hague Conventions – how effective was it? Did it justify, and did its results reward, the heavy investment of human skill and dedication which went into its making? Have the Geneva and Hague Conventions (taking them together, as we now may, as converging branches of international humanitarian law) proved worthwhile?

The first thing one observes as one surveys this body of law is the limitation of its scope; in particular that, until after 1945, very little of it was concerned with 'civilians'. Since 1945, it has become a commonplace that civilians are the category of persons most in need of whatever protection an up-dated law of war can offer; and it is towards that end that has been directed much of the thrust of the last ten years' intense activity in respect of the reaffirmation and development of the law of war. What happened to civilians earlier? And what happened by the end of the Second World War to create the ineffaceable impression that a more systematic regard for them was long overdue?

The theory about civilians from early days (i.e. since eighteenth-century writers began systematically to take note of them, in the age of 'limited wars') was that civilians were best kept right out of it. Wars, they maintained, were properly fought by 'armies'; by armed forces anyway, whether regulars or militiamen, raised by states for the special business of armed conflict and prudently controlled therein. No eighteenth-century government put arms into the hands of its subjects if it could help it. Just as it was desirable not to arm civilians, so to the mind of the eighteenth-century writers it was not necessary to harm them either. They rarely got in the way of the fighting unless they were unlucky enough to inhabit a village which became part of the battlefield or a fortified town which became besieged. Humanitarianism chimed in nicely with official self-interest to recommend the observance of a distinction between combatants and non-combatants. Non-combatants were of more value to all parties if they were allowed to carry on with their own business as peasants, traders, merchants etc. They were of more value to armies because you could get more out of a civilian populace by regulated requisitioning than by wasteful looting and vengeful destruction, which moreover was bad for discipline besides provoking resistance. Non-combatants were of more value to governments because their freedom and security kept in better shape the wealth-producing sectors of society upon whom governments and governing élites ultimately rested, whether they were winners or losers. Furthermore, there might not be much point in a victor's acquisition of territory which had been devastated and depopulated.

So the law of war in those formulative years of the eighteenth and early nineteenth centuries prescribed as fundamental that distinction between combatant and non-combatant which ever since has been a central part of it, and military practice then found it not too difficult to observe. This was because armies were so much smaller than they became after the French Revolution, because they were often under rigid and effective discipline, and because their systematic provisioning had become an expert and prominent if laborious part of the business of conducting military operations. But although it was not too difficult to keep non-combatants out of it in the way prescribed, it was not too easy either. Let us now examine more closely the situations in which the civilian was inexorably caught up in the wheels of war, taking the least lethal first.

First then, requisitions. Even in their own countries, armies on the move in the eighteenth and nineteenth century had legal power to requisition what they imperatively needed for their maintenance and movement: horses, fodder, lodgings, and victuals; and it was all carefully laid down how the civilian, who had to provide these things and thereby lost money, could be reimbursed and indemnified. In an enemy's country, armies of course would just take what they needed; nevertheless requisitions were expected to be made in an orderly and regulated style for the reasons already given: that such a style of requisitioning actually ensured better and longer-lasting supplies, and avoided driving the population to resistance. By the same reasoning, armies that could afford it (like Wellington's, conspicuously, in Spain and southern France in 1813–14) found it more advantageous to dispense with requisitioning altogether and simply to pay on the nail for what they needed. Throughout the nineteenth century requisitions remained a touchy topic. Here was a war-practice which caused inconvenience and loss to civilians, quite contrary to the theory as the more pacifistic publicists understood it. The peace movement of the nineteenth century and the internationalist movement with which it largely overlapped had their representatives and sympathizers in the debate about the proper development of the international law of war. To those generally non-war-minded and commercially-interested people, this requisitioning activity of the military seemed highly offensive; and since they were capable of as extreme a demand as that enemy private property on enemy ships at sea should be free from capture in time of war, it was no surprise that they were capable also of pressing for a law of land war to restrain invading and occupying armies from requisitioning anything except by receipt in due form signed by a superior officer, etc.

But not only the 'peace people' had a personal or professional interest in this matter. It also mattered very much to the spokesmen of the small countries which were liable to suffer occupation: Belgium and the Netherlands above all. Requisitions were among the major topics thoroughly debated at the 1874 Brussels Conference on the Law of Land War and both Hague Conferences. The military representatives of the big powers, who were going to be doing the occupying, there sought with considerable patience to persuade the representatives of the small powers that there were limits to the time which a brigade of hungry and footsore soldiers could wait in enemy country while their senior officers negotiated with the businessmen and the officials of local authorities in the territory they were invading.[13] Military necessity, in its mildest form, thus pressed somewhat heavily on the civilian in an invaded and occupied territory, and could not avoid doing so.

The second and more serious situation in which a civilian found the line between himself and the combatant less clear than he might like, was when he was inside a fortified or defended place which was being bombarded. The authorities on the developing law of war during the eighteenth and nineteenth centuries agreed that it was regrettable (though they could not agree that it was worse than that) when civilians understandably suffered from the bombardment of legitimate military targets; the list of which was to become extended through the years from the walls, forts, and magazines of defended places to include railway installations, factories, government offices, and so on. What however was alleged by some authorities to be clearly unlawful was the bombarding of civilians inside defended places with a view to make them suffer and complain and so to hasten (thus ran the military man's hopes) the place's surrender.

The arguments used to sustain this contention were as usual mixed. They were partly humanitarian but they could also be utilitarian and tactical, inasmuch as such bombardments were believed by many to be ineffective, even counter-productive. The Germans went in a good deal for bombardments of this kind in the 1870–1 war, but neither then nor at any other times earlier or later, has bombardment been clearly seen to have worked as its protagonists hoped and intended. This calls our attention to the fact that one motive for such bombardments can be punitive and vindictive. For instance, there was undoubtedly a good deal of such motivation behind the aerial bombardments of both World Wars, which provided a convenient outlet for pent-up popular passion. When did the progress of military technology make possible such popular political uses of bombardment? One can see something of it in the British bombardments and devastations along the east coast of the United States in the war of 1812–14. It is manifestly present in the glee with which the North in the American Civil War followed Sherman's devastation of Georgia, and only a few years later it was visible again in the popular pressure put upon the German High Command to bombard Paris in the winter of 1870–1.[14] In this case, as in the two others cited, the bombarders' theory went beyond the 'tactical' to a more radical 'strategic' argument: that such violence against civilians was justified on the ground that, in more or less democratic states, civilians were involved in responsibility for causing and conducting war, and should therefore be prepared to feel what war was really like. Sherman was quite explicit about this, as the British admirals had been before him; and so also were Bismarck and the

German generals, whose objections to bombardment were not so much that the French republicans did not richly deserve it as that bombardment was not the most effective or economical way to achieve the military objects sought. Long therefore before the development of aircraft made long-distance strategic bombing possible, the juridical (or legalistic) theory to justify it and the national passion to demand it were both already there. From the First World War onwards, bombardment, so long a controversial topic in the history of the development (or paralysis) of the law of war, became more particularly a part of the history of air warfare, and has to be left by the present author to the other contributors to this book.

There remains the third and worst of the situations which made difficult the maintenance of that distinction between combatant and non-combatant which is crucial to our theme. This is the situation where a people offers resistance to an invader or occupier and/or when partisan or guerrilla warfare is conducted against him. Here we come to the heart of the contemporary problem in respect of the law of land war. The accommodation of guerrilla warfare within the law of war has been the biggest of its problems since the Second World War, and is so still. What is its history, and what are its constituents?

The history is curious. The majority of international law writers, from 1815 to 1945, whether they were 'civilian' or 'military', seem to have regarded it as a problem which ought not to have existed and which they hoped would go away.[15] It was also a problem the consideration of which involved more than the usual amount of 'double-think' which is always present whenever there is discussion of laws bearing unequally on different parties.[16] We need go back no further than the Revolutionary and Napoleonic wars. In them there was of course a great deal of national resistance, guerrilla war, and war of national liberation. The Spanish people's war against the French is the best known of these episodes but there were many more. Within Revolutionary France itself there was the Civil War based on the Vendée; there was fierce popular resistance to the French in parts of Italy and in the Austrian Tyrol; the Russian expulsion of the great French invasion was

achieved partly through guerrilla resistance; and the Prussian
patriotic rising of 1813 offered another and, all things Prussian
considered, rather surprising piece of evidence that the same
spirit of national resistance was operative there as well.
'Double-think' comes into the case because so few of the
regular and high-placed military who were concerned with
the development of the law of war thereafter were willing to
admit that what was sauce for the goose was sauce also for the
gander: i.e. that if popular resistance and partisan warfare
were all right as methods of defending your own country
against a neighbour, they must be all right equally for the
neighbour when defending his country against yours.[17]

In this tendency towards applying a double standard of
judgement we meet, I suggest, an unintended revival of
classical just war theory, the importance of which had steadily
diminished in the writings of international lawyers about war
during the Enlightenment. Some medieval and early modern
writers had maintained that a belligerent conducting a just
war could do things which would be unlawful if done by an
enemy who, by definition, was conducting an unjust war. This
theory of course led only to aggravated nastiness in war for
the obvious reason that no belligerent can think of himself and
his cause as anything but just. Sensibly, therefore, the
developers of the international law of war after Grotius edged
away from the just/unjust war definition, at any rate in respect
of the actual conduct of war, during that very period of years
when the law of war was being developed emphatically as one
for wars conducted by regular armed forces who could be
instructed in it and disciplined to observe it. Since moreover
the guerrilla side of the Revolutionary and Napoleonic Wars
was the source of most of their atrocity stories, humanitarians
in the nineteenth century were ready to support the
professional military in placing guerrilla warfare beyond the
legal pale; and this despite the fact that guerrilla war had
been part of every invaded state's defence efforts in those
heroic years, and the exploits of guerrilla fighters were from
that time onwards among the most colourful in the popular
literature of nineteenth-century patriotism. Hence that element of 'double-think' nicely summarized in the exchange

between Favre and Bismarck during the peace negotiations of early 1871. Favre complained that the Germans had acted with unreasonable severity against French partisans since they, the Germans, had engaged in partisan activities against the French in 1813. Bismarck rejoined that indeed the Germans had done so, and that there could still be seen, in Prussia, the marks on the trees where the French had hanged them.[18]

The Franco-Prussian war brought the questions of resistance and guerrilla warfare to the forefront of the debate about the law of war, then entering its phase of most intensive development. The Germans disliked the French *francs tireurs* at least as much as conventional regular-led armies always have done, and made it their main grievance against the French, that the war which ought to have been over with the surrenders at Sedan and Metz had dragged on miserably through the winter and become as unpleasant and vindictive an affair as guerrilla operations must always tend to make it. This became a kind of obsession with German military writers to the extent that, when Belgium was invaded in 1914, the greater part of the German army so much expected to meet *franc-tireur* resistance action (the Walloon Belgians being francophone and Catholic) that they saw *francs tireurs* behind everything that went amiss or could not be explained, and did some dreadful things as a result.[19]

Through all the discussions and conferences that went on between 1870 and the First World War, the German voice was, I judge, the loudest in arguing that guerrilla warfare and what we would now call 'total national defence' were incompatible with the restraints which it is the purpose of the law of war to set on military operations; their main argument being the standard one that, unless an occupying army can be sure who the enemy combatants are, it cannot restrain itself from severities against all who might be combatants or might be helping them. But these arguments were not put by German representatives alone. Between the Germans and the Russians there appeared, on this as on most other matters, little difference. Indeed the Russo-German case, as we might fairly call it, was not unreasonable. Russia's chief representa-

tive at Brussels in 1874, Baron Jomini, temperately rejected
the charge that it paralysed the rights of defence, declaring:

This reproach is unfounded. It would be giving the lie to the most glorious
recollections of Russia. But war has altered its character. Formerly it was a
kind of drama, in which personal strength and courage played a prominent
part; individuality has in the present day been replaced by formidable
machinery put into action by genius and science. It becomes, therefore,
necessary, if one may use the expression, to regulate the inspirations of
patriotism. Otherwise, in opposing irregular bodies of enthusiasts to
powerfully organized armies, the risk of compromising national defence
and of rendering it more fatal to the country itself than to the invader would
be incurred.

Germany's chief representative, General Voigts-Rhetz, supported this view of the matter, 'disclaiming any wish to put
obstacles in the way of the levée en masse, a mode of defence
which he declared to be legitimate, and sometimes necessary.
It was against the abuses to which it may lead that he
contended.'[20]

Against this cool professional military orthodoxy the
Belgians and the Dutch (supported by the Norwegians and to
a great extent the Swiss and the British) argued with
interesting passion. The British representative, General
Horsford, who seems to have noted very closely the proceedings
of which his instructions made him a passive observer,
reported them thus:

No country could possibly admit ... that if a population of a *de facto*
occupied district should rise in arms against the established authority they
should be subjected to the laws of war in force in the occupying army. He
(M. de Lansberge) admitted that in time of war necessity might occasionally
force the occupier to treat with rigour a population which might rise, and
that on account of its weakness the population would be forced to submit.
But the idea of delivering over, in advance, to the justice of the enemy those
men who, from patriotic motives and at their own peril, expose themselves
to all the dangers consequent upon a rising is, he remarked, one which no
Government would dare to entertain. Baron Lambermont (of Belgium)
... concluded by saying that if the citizens were to be sacrificed for having
attempted to defend their country at the risk of their lives, they need not
find inscribed on the post at the foot of which they were to be shot, the
Article of a Treaty signed by their own Government which had in advance
condemned them to death.[21]

The same story, the same theoretical battle, repeated themselves at The Hague; with the same result.[22] The Hague Rules made little room for the guerrilla fighter, and displayed no sympathy towards populations which might rise in arms against an occupying power. This defect in the law of war, if it was one, was not much, if at all, noticed during the First World War. There was no guerrilla fighting on the western front and although there was some in the east, it seems to have attracted very little – one may say, *surprisingly* little – attention from the international-law writers afterwards. (I must here confess that I have not been able to study the Russian writers.) The law remained unchanged through the twenties and thirties, and I have not so far found it suggested by any of the commentators of that period that guerrilla warfare needed to be dealt with. Aerial bombardment, submarines, gas, and to some extent civilians were the topics that were most discussed by the experts and the interested amateurs between the wars, not guerrillas.

Their day came after the Second World War, when resistance movements and guerrilla operations were so many and, militarily, so significant. It became a matter of political necessity as well as juridical common sense to enlarge the protection of the Geneva Conventions to include at any rate 'respectable' guerrillas. The 1949 Conventions went some distance in this direction; a lot further than some powers liked (especially Britain and France), but not far enough, as it has appeared, for the needs of national liberation movements in general. In 1977, at the Geneva Conference, we may have witnessed the success of a kind of united guerrilla front; at last the guerrilla may feel he is as legitimate a warrior as any other.*

But what of the civilian? How legitimate is he? What will the new version of the Geneva Conventions do for him? No one could doubt, when the war ended in 1945, that the main defect of the law of war lay in its failure to protect civilians. They had suffered badly for two reasons: first, the usual problems presented by guerrilla war and national resistance

---

* See pp. 135–60 below.

movements; second, the ruthless policies which the German and Soviet armed forces had had to apply, whether they liked them or not. It was painfully clear by 1945 that civilians in occupied territories could no longer expect to benefit from those restraints which the law of land war before 1914 had to a small extent imposed and to a larger extent assumed. In 1949, a new Geneva Convention was produced for the protection of civilians. How far it has worked well or badly, is not for me to inquire. Nor dare we prophesy about the future – except perhaps to wonder whether the new-style law of war will give civilians any better protection from the operations of guerrillas, than it was found to give them from the operations of regular soldiers. Or should we pose the simple question: has the civilian, as liberal Europe used to know him, become extinct?

NOTES

1. Maurice Baring, *Royal Flying Corps Headquarters, 1914–1918* (London, 1920), pp. 55–6.
2. John Reed, *Insurgent Mexico* (New York, 1914), pp. 142–3.
3. See e.g. his Instructions for the Academy of Nobles, cited by P. E. Corbett, *Law and Society in the Relations of States* (New York, 1951), pp. 85–6.
4. He referred to this in several speeches during November and December 1777. See Basil Williams, *Life of William Pitt* (London, 1913. 1915 edn.), II, 319–25.
   The relevant part of the 20 November oration is given in *The Oxford Book of English Prose*, ed. A. Quiller-Couch (Oxford, 1925), no. 258.
5. 'Introduction to the Proceedings of the Committee for cloathing French Prisoners of War', in *Works of Samuel Johnson: a new edition in twelve volumes* (London, 1820), II, 368–70.
6. Pierre Boissier, *De Solférino à Tsouschima . . .* (Paris, 1963), pp. 188–212 gives a useful sketch of these conventional improvements of the eighteenth and early nineteenth centuries.
7. There is massive testimony to this judgement as to the relative showings of the two sides. Henry Dunant himself pronounced it (e.g. in his address, on 6 August 1872, to the National Association for the Promotion of Social Science, published that year, as a pamphlet – it was not included in the Association's annual Transactions). Gustave Moynier, his successor at the centre, dealt with it fully in his 1873 pamphlet *La Convention de Genève pendant la guerre franco-allemande*. The

other richest source of information is Rolin-Jaequemyn's articles in the *Revue de Droit International*, II (1870), 643 ff., III (1871), 288 ff., and IV (1872), 481 ff.

8. A full expression of the German view may be found in M. Schmidt-Ernsthansen, *Das Prinzip der Genfer Convention ... und der freiwilligen nationalen Hülfsorganisation für den Krieg* (Berlin, 1874). A useful dispassionate review by W. G. Macpherson is in the *Journal of the Royal Army Medical Corps*, Nov. 1910.

9. The story is told by Pierre Boissier, op. cit., p. 413. There is a curious wall-painting of it in the Institut Henry-Dunant at Geneva.

10. Conrad, 'Aristocracy and War', 1905, in *Notes on Life and Letters* (London, 1921), p. 143.

11. Cited by B. V. A. Röling, *International Law in an Expanded World* (Amsterdam, 1960), p. 27.

12. *House of Lords Weekly Hansard*, vol. 376, no. 987, column 1521. (The wording is not significantly different from that in *The Times*.)

13. See especially the expostulations of General Voigts-Rhetz on 20 August, in (e.g.) *British Parliamentary Papers*, 1875, LXXXII, pp. 435–43.

14. Michael Howard, *The Franco-Prussian War* (London, 1960. 1967 edn.), on p. 356, n. 4 cites a popular jingle with the catchy chorus, 'Bumm! Bumm! Bumm!'.

15. Such is my judgement of the literature so far studied. Certainly voices were now and then heard on the other side. The most that could be made of them was made by the eminent Soviet jurist, I. P. Trainin, in a 1945 article 'Questions of Guerrilla Warfare in the Law of War', trans. and published in *American Journal of International Law* vol. XI (1946), pp. 534–62.

16. *Chambers Twentieth Century Dictionary* (1972 edn.): 'Double-think, the faculty of simultaneously harbouring two conflicting beliefs – coined by George Orwell in his *Nineteen Eighty-Four* (1949).'

17. Michel Veuthey, *Guérilla et droit humanitaire* (Geneva 1976), p. 37, n. 74 pertinently cites Field-Marshal Lord Montgomery: 'one side's resistance hero is the other side's terrorist or bandit'.

18. Related by Howard, op. cit., p. 251.

19. This explanation of most of what happened at Louvain, offered by some from the very beginning, but denied in the official German account, has been scientifically established by P. Schöller, *Der Fall Löwen und der Weissbuch* (Köln–Graz, 1958); translated as *Le Cas de Louvain ...* (Louvain and Paris, 1958).

20. *British Parliamentary Papers*, op. cit., pp. 365–6.

21. Foreign Office 'Confidential Print' (F.O. 881) 2542, letter no. 38, Horsford to Lord Derby, 21 Aug. 1874.

22. The course of discussion can be followed in John Brown Scott (ed.), *Proceedings of the Hague Conferences: The Conference of 1899* (New York, 1920), pp. 526–55; and *Reports to the Hague Conferences of 1899 and 1907* (Oxford, 1917), pp. 149–54.

3

RESTRAINTS ON WAR AT SEA
BEFORE 1945
Bryan Ranft

Introduction

In the long history of attempts to restrain war on land it would
be surprising to find serious consideration ever having been
given to the formulation of international agreements forbid-
ding armies to kill their opponents or invade enemy territory.
Yet it is arguable that the most consistent attempts made
before 1945 to control war at sea would, if the restraints they
postulated had been fully applied, have had an equivalent
effect in nullifying naval warfare as an instrument of national
policy, as would those prohibiting the killing of combatants
and the occupation of territory in land warfare. This is
because the most important of these proposed restraints were
directed towards minimizing the economic damage and loss of
non-combatants' lives in maritime war by putting severe
limitations on the rights of belligerents to direct their naval
operations against merchant shipping, its cargoes, passengers,
and crews. The acceptance of such restraints raised fundamental questions about the utility of maritime strategy and
operations.

For a maritime nation such as Britain, the destruction of an
enemy's maritime trade was seen as its main, and sometimes
its only, weapon against a strong continental enemy.
Conversely, for a Britain with her national prosperity and
later her national existence dependent upon the continuance
of maritime trade in wartime, the possibility of its being made
immune from enemy attacks had apparent attractions. For
weaker naval powers such as France and Germany, who were
also strong continental powers, attacks on sea-borne trade
could be their only method of attacking a maritime enemy's
unacceptable dominance at sea. Nations which remained
neutral and wished to take advantage of the commercial

opportunities offered by war, claimed that the immunity of their ships and cargoes from naval operations was a natural and legal right. For the United States in particular this was seen as a vital part of the whole concept of neutrality.

Of a different order was the impact of technological change, not only on navies but on society at large. Were international agreements to restrict naval operations, arrived at in the days of sail and when wars had a limited effect on national survival, likely to remain acceptable after the advent of the mine, the submarine, and the aircraft, and of wars demanding the total mobilization of the belligerents' human and economic resources? Or, putting the question more widely: in wars where defeat was identified with the complete destruction of the state, was it rational to expect governments to adhere to agreements arrived at in totally different circumstances? Arising from this was the problem which faced belligerents of calculating whether the casting aside of hitherto accepted international restraints on operations against merchant shipping would be so certain a way to victory that it would be worth risking the irritation of neutrals, perhaps to the extent of their becoming enemies.

These general problems and the more detailed ones arising from them are so central to an understanding of the attempts to impose restraints on maritime war as to justify concentrating entirely on them, and only to note in passing that the purely humanitarian restraints on war identified in the various Geneva and Hague Conventions were held to be applicable to war at sea.[1] Whether they were adhered to or not, depended upon their implications for the broader issues outlined above.

The Organic Connection between Naval Policy and Warfare and Maritime Trade

In the western world until the late seventeenth century, with the exception of the galley fleets of the Mediterranean, there was no fundamental distinction between fighting and trading vessels. Until the late nineteenth century, mercantile and fishing fleets were seen as nurseries of seamen for the fighting fleet. In other words, commercial ships and their crews were an integral part of a nation's capability to wage maritime war. Throughout the age of Mercantilism, trade was seen as a limited commodity, which had to be won and protected from rivals if the nation were to prosper. This concept was most clearly formulated in the Anglo–Dutch wars of the seventeenth century and cogently expressed by Samuel Pepys's sea-going merchant friend Captain Cocke, 'Whoe discoursed well of the good effects in some kind of a Dutch war and conquest . . . That is, the trade of the world is too little for us two, therefore one must down.'[2] It is symbolic of this organic connection between maritime trade, national prosperity, and naval warfare that the three Anglo–Dutch wars, in which the two protagonists' major aim was the destruction of their enemy's trade and the protection and increase of their own, were also the wars in which three central concepts of naval warfare were for the first time fully recognized. The need to fight for command of the sea, the primacy of the battle-fleet for securing this command, and that the greatest benefit from gaining such command was the ability to sweep your enemy's merchantmen from the sea and give security to your own, were the principles which emerged from the experience. As long as Mercantilism prevailed, it was inevitable that the destruction, or better still, the capture of an enemy's merchant shipping and its cargoes should remain an essential part of naval operations, and that effective restraints on such operations would be unacceptable to strong maritime powers.

Another factor working against the acceptance of such restraints was that as wars became longer and more likely to be waged by coalitions of powers and fighting-forces of increasing size and cost, the importance of sea-borne trade in supplying and financing them became more, and on occasion decisively, significant. The strategic implications of Britain's economic warfare against Napoleon, based on her maritime predominance, was a supreme demonstration of this.[3]

Despite all this, it did seem in the second half of the nineteenth century, with the advent of Free Trade and *laisser-faire* economics, that the organic connection between maritime war and trade might be broken or at least reduced in importance. On paper, considerable progress was made in limiting naval operations against merchant shipping. This will be analysed later; but no sooner had the trend appeared than a contrary influence began to manifest itself. This came first in the realization that in future wars industrial production would be of equal significance to military strength and that therefore raw materials for factories and food for industrial workers could be considered legitimate objects for attack at sea.[4] Secondly there came a belief, expressed first in France and then in Germany, that the advent of steam propulsion, more effective naval artillery, and the revolutionary effect of underwater weapons, coinciding with the now complete dependence of nations such as Britain upon sea-borne supplies, had made a ruthlessly waged war against merchant shipping potentially strategically decisive, instead of the ancillary operation it had been in earlier times.

When the First World War came these two factors combined to sweep aside the elaborate pattern of international restraints which had been accepted by the major powers between 1856 and 1909. This process was to be repeated in the Second World War, when the inter-war attempts to prevent a recurrence of the unrestricted submarine warfare of 1917–18 were jettisoned, virtually from the outbreak of hostilities.

If the facts of economic and technological development were thus to set up an insurmountable barrier to the imposition of effective restraints on war at sea, and even to make naval operations against non-combatants more ruthless than before, the systematic study of maritime war embodied in the work of A. T. Mahan and Julian Corbett[5] was to re-emphasize in the minds of European statesmen and public opinion the permanence of the organic relationship between maritime trade and naval war. Corbett's *Some Principles of Maritime Strategy*, published in 1911 and embodying his teaching to the Royal Naval War College, gave the fullest expression of this. To Corbett, the whole purpose of naval operations, including fleet actions, was to gain control of sea communications:

By occupying [an enemy's] maritime communications and closing the points of distribution in which they terminate, we destroy the national life afloat and therefore check the vitality of that life ashore, as far as one is dependent on the other. As long as we retain the power and the right to stop maritime communications, the analogy between command of the sea and the conquest of territory is very close.[6]

He saw the prevention of enemy trade rather than the destruction of ships and cargoes as the desirable objective, and one which could only be attained if a naval power having achieved command of the sea maintains 'the right to forbid . . . the passage of both public and private property upon the sea.' He further argued that for a maritime power to sacrifice such a right would be as illogical as for a military power to relinquish the right to occupy towns and ports and to impose requisitions of goods and financial levies in land warfare.[7]

Developments in Attempts to Restrain Belligerent Operations Against Sea-borne Trade[8]

These developments centred on six main issues:

1. The immunity of neutral ships and cargoes.
2. The treatment of enemy goods in neutral ships.
3. The treatment of neutral goods in belligerent ships.
4. The definition of contraband of war.
5. The validity of blockade.
6. The acceptance of the total immunity of private property, whether it belonged to belligerents or neutrals.

Before the Declaration of Paris in 1856 there was no uniformity of theory or practice on these issues. European powers, and later the United States,[9] adopted views in accordance with their perceived interests at particular times. The only generally accepted agreement was that distinctions in treatment should be applied between belligerent and neutral ships and cargoes. There was no similar convergence of views on discriminating between the public and private ships and goods of belligerents.

From the mid-seventeenth century the Dutch, with their aim of becoming the greatest of sea traders and carriers, pressed for the widest possible restraints on naval operations against trade, on the principle that a neutral flag should protect all goods carried, including those of belligerents. Britain on the contrary, confident of her ability to sweep enemy merchant shipping off the seas, was determined that the pressure this placed on her adversaries should not be relieved by the arrival of supplies in neutral ships. The United States from its foundation, seeing itself as a permanent neutral in European wars, and determined to oppose all obstacles to its economic growth, argued for the imposition of the strongest possible restraints on belligerents' interference with neutrals' ships and goods. She also argued for the strictest possible limitation of contraband to goods solely of a military character. During the Napoleonic wars this was extended to pressure for the complete abolition of the concept of contraband and the assertion of the natural right of neutrals to provide arms and munitions to all belligerents who wished to buy them.

The United States, while admitting the right of a belligerent to impose a blockade, insisted that she would only recognize as legal blockades those where the presence of adequate naval forces virtually guaranteed the interception of ships trying to enter blockaded ports. She particularly objected to general declarations of blockade such as were made by Britain in the Napoleonic wars. Finally, it was to be the United States, as will be shown later, which initiated discussion of the most sweeping restraint of all: the granting of immunity from seizure of all private, as distinct from state-owned, ships and cargoes, belligerent as well as neutral.

The Declaration of Paris,[10] which was based on the practice of Britain and France in the Crimean War, marked a notable advance in the international acceptance of restraints. It had four major provisions:

1. The abolition of privateering. This removed what had been one of the most dangerous threats to merchant shipping in past wars.
2. Belligerents' goods in neutral ships to be immune from capture, if they were not contraband.
3. Neutrals' goods in belligerent ships to be immune from capture, if they were not contraband.

4. Blockade in order to be internationally binding must be effective.

Although these last three provisions gave international acceptance to restraints long urged by the United States, she alone of the major maritime powers refused to adhere to the Declaration, because she could not accept the abolition of privateering. The United States Government's instructions to its minister in London in 1854 emphasized that it was 'not prepared to listen to any proposition for a total suppression of privateering. It would not enter into any convention whereby it would preclude itself from resorting to the mercantile marine of the country, in case it should become a belligerent party.' It further urged that the abolition of privateering would only be to the advantage of strong naval powers as it would enable them to dispense with the allocation of warships for the defence of trade and use them for offensive operations. The only conditions on which the United States would consider abolition would be if the other maritime powers accepted her ultimate aim of securing the complete immunity of all private ships and cargoes in future naval wars.[11] This, together with the results of the omission from the Declaration of Paris of any substantial definition of contraband, were to be the main issues in attempts to develop further restraints before 1914.

Further Pressures to Make Private Property Immune from Capture at Sea

There was a wide range of forces working in this direction. The ideological belief among the influential commercial classes of the industrialized world that the free flow of trade was essential to the spread of civilization led them to assert that it should not be obstructed by war, which was a regrettable survival from a more barbarous age. The growth in the economic and political importance of the United States which had long advocated the imposition of this final restraint gave increasing support to those demanding it. In Europe, the conviction grew among land powers, Prussia among them,[12] that in view of their relative naval weakness they would have more to gain from immunity than from the slight pressures they could bring to bear on strong maritime nations by attacking their trade. Most surprisingly of all, in Britain, hitherto the leading opponent of such limitation of the use of naval power, there began to be heard Parliamentary and commercial demands that she should surrender her traditional maritime rights. Although complete acceptance of these demands was successfully resisted by the Admiralty and successive governments, the Declaration of London in 1909 saw Britain accepting the immunity of so wide a range of goods from being classed as contraband as to go a considerable way towards the United States' point of view.

It is worthwhile looking in some detail at the development of American and British thinking on this issue, not only for its intrinsic interest but also because it was to be a major cause of serious disagreement between the two nations, before and during the First World War, and even more so during the immediate post-war years – a disagreement which crystallized in Woodrow Wilson's campaign for 'The Freedom of the Seas', a slogan acidly described by Sir Julian Corbett as 'One of those ringing phrases which haunt the ear and continue to confuse judgement.'[13]

American pronouncements on the subject go back to the early years of the Republic and provide fine examples of the dual basis of moral rectitude and economic advantage which so often characterized her foreign policy. In 1793 Jefferson, protesting against a British Order in Council authorizing the seizure of food ships bound from the United States to France, claimed that nations which keep aloof from war 'retain their natural right to pursue their agriculture, manufactures and other ordinary vocations, to carry the produce of their industry for exchange to all other nations, belligerent or neutral, as usual'. It was a concession from this natural right to allow belligerents to institute a blockade and try to prevent munitions of war recognized as contraband from reaching the enemy, but food could not be declared contraband as Britain now seemed to be claiming: 'We see then a practice begun

... which strikes at the root of our agriculture, that branch of industry which gives food, clothing and comfort to the great mass of the inhabitants of these states.'[14] In 1823 Secretary Adams pressed the British Government to accept a Convention aimed at 'the perpetual abolition of private war upon the seas', on the grounds of 'the same precepts of justice, charity and of peace under which Christian nations had by common consent exempted private property on land from destruction in war'. Despite his arguments that this would be to Britain's advantage by saving her the enormous expense of providing naval protection for her increasing maritime trade, five years of negotiation produced no results.[15]

The American government took up the cudgels again during the negotiations which produced the Declaration of Paris, arguing that if all private property were made exempt from capture this would effectively restrain behaviour which had led to so much friction in the past: 'The Right of Search which has been the source of so much annoyance and so many injuries to neutral commerce, would be effectively restricted to such cases only as justified a suspicion of an attempt to trade with places actually in a state of siege or blockade.'[16] This also reflected the view that the only legitimate blockades were those closing ports in the theatres of war. General economic blockade of a country would not be recognized by the United States.

Despite the fact that the American Government's main reason for refusing to adhere to the Declaration of Paris was its objection to the abolition of privateering, it is worth noting that in its war with Spain in 1898 it did not resort to privateering and in practice observed the other terms of the Declaration.[17]

The United States continued to press for the immunity of private property and the most limited definition of contraband possible in the years before 1914. Her delegations at the Hague Conferences of 1899 and 1907 were specifically instructed to work to these ends, but with no immediate success.[18] Yet in 1909 the Declaration of London was to go a long way to achieving the second aim, thanks to a surprising change of attitude by Britain.

Great Britain's Attitude to the Immunity of Private Property after the Declaration of Paris

Successive British governments held that although adherence to the Declaration had meant making substantial concessions to neutrals, the abolition of privateering was an acceptable compensation. Moreover, the continuation of the right to impose blockade and to define contraband at the beginning of a war, combined with Britain's geographical position relative to the Continent, would still enable her to use her sea power effectively against a European enemy. The maintenance of these remaining belligerent rights was seen by the greater part of political and public opinion, and of course the Admiralty, as vital to national survival.

Gradually however an opposing minority view began to emerge, shared by Radicals in Parliament and some sections of the commercial community. This was that the naval advantages were far outweighed by the vulnerability of Britain's own maritime trade in war, and that they should be surrendered in favour of the great economic benefits which would come from international agreement to exempt all private property at sea from capture. Advocates of this policy tried to win round naval opinion by urging that, freed from the necessity to protect merchant shipping, the Navy would be able to concentrate on its proper task of destroying the enemy battle-fleet. Such arguments did not prevail over the more traditional ones but support for them in the Parliamentary Liberal Party, particularly from Lord Chancellor Loreburn, and among the Party's commercial supporters, led to Asquith's government taking the lead in the negotiations which in 1909 produced the Declaration of London.[19]

These negotiations emerged from a Convention accepted at the Second Hague Peace Conference of 1907 which established an international tribunal to consider appeals from the findings of national prize courts. This in itself was a noteworthy acceptance of an international restraint on what had hitherto been accepted as a purely national prerogative. It also necessitated the formulation of rules by which the new international court should operate. This was to be the work of a conference in London in which the British Government took the initiative in producing a Declaration, denounced by the Secretary of the Committee of Imperial Defence, Captain Maurice Hankey, as inimical to British interests because it filled in the loopholes left by the Declaration of Paris, particularly those relating to blockade and contraband.[20]

Henceforward, blockade to be acceptable to neutrals must be 'effective'; which was defined as demanding a continuous close guard of enemy ports. Contraband was made subject to detailed definition and classification. Only goods which were solely of military use were to be treated as absolute contraband. Goods which had both military and civil utility were to be defined as conditional contraband, and liable to seizure only if it could be established that they were destined for enemy territory and intended for military use. A third category of free goods was established which covered a long list of articles which were never to be treated as contraband.[21]

The acceptance of these restraints by Britain was full of contradictions. The emergence of mines, torpedoes, and long-range coastal artillery had made close blockade of enemy ports impossible. The inclusion in the list of conditional contraband of items such as gold and bullion; railway materials; fuel and lubricants, and many other articles of great military utility, was made even more unacceptable by the further limitation that such conditional contraband could not be seized if it were destined for a neutral port, without any account being taken of the possibility of its being taken on into enemy territory by land transport. Even more unrealistic was the inclusion in the free list of items such as textiles, rubber, and chemicals, all of which had direct military utility.

Behind these detailed contradictions was a much more fundamental one stressed by Hankey and the Conservative opponents to Britain's acceptance of the Declaration.[22] At the very time when the country was becoming aware of the real danger of a war with Germany and beginning to plan for the eventuality, it was absurd for her to be sacrificing the maritime belligerent rights which all her history had shown to be the major means of applying economic pressure to a continental opponent. Or, putting it in more general terms and thinking of Britain's vulnerability as well as of her naval strength, it was illusory, at a time when technological development had made it inevitable that any future war should involve the whole human and industrial resources of belligerents, to expect that a nation which had the means of waging effective economic warfare would refrain from doing so, whatever international agreements she might have signed in peacetime.

In the event, Conservative objections to the Declaration led to its ratification being rejected by the House of Lords. When war came in 1914 Britain firmly resisted American pressures to accept its restraints, although Germany initially did so.[23] As the war progressed Britain's naval power, combined with her economic and political influence, enabled her virtually to cut off neutral sea-borne trade with Germany. After 1918 so strong was the British conviction that this had been her unique contribution to the defeat of the enemy and the vindication of her otherwise under-used sea power, that the calls from President Wilson and his successors for Britain to accept the 'Freedom of the Seas' and the strengthening of neutral as compared with belligerent rights, produced very little response. At the beginning of the Second World War there was no avoidable delay in putting into effect naval, political, and economic measures designed ultimately once again to isolate Germany from sea-borne supplies.[24]

Naturally such British policies, which during the First World War in particular seemed to reject all the apparent progress which had been made to limit the effects of maritime war on maritime trade, led to strong protests from neutrals, with the United States at their head. But any possibility that this could lead to a neutral combination against Britain was removed by Germany's more objectionable rejection in both world wars of the imagined progress which had been made to safeguard the lives of civilians, the passengers and crews of merchant ships, neutral and belligerent alike, by her use of the submarine as her major naval weapon against Britain.[25]

This is a well-known story; but new light can be cast upon it by looking at it against the dual background of the French *Jeune École* of naval warfare and the impact of technical change on the internationally accepted right of belligerent warships to visit and search merchantmen on the high seas.

The French Jeune École[26]

This group of French publicists and naval men, which achieved prominence between the 1880s and the turn of the century, advocated a theory of maritime war which totally rejected any restrictions on naval operations against merchant shipping. The school was animated by extreme Anglophobia, and convinced that Britain could be defeated by war against the merchant shipping upon which her very survival now depended. Such a war could be decisive as it had never been in the past, because the new naval technology in the form of fast light cruisers and torpedo-boats would enable France to inflict unacceptable losses, if only she were willing to use ruthless surprise attacks without paying heed to the safety of passengers and crews. The school's first publicist Gabriel Charmes, in his *La Réforme de la marine* (1886), saw the essence of France's new approach to naval war as being 'to fall without pity on the weak; and without shame and all possible speed to fly from the strong.'[27] In 1893 the textbook of the movement, *Essaie de stratégie navale,* was to assert that in modern war it was no greater crime to sink a merchantman or bombard a coastal town than it was to destroy a warship.[28] Even the more responsible Lanessan, a former Minister of Marine, spoke in 1903 of the likelihood of merchantmen being sunk on sight by torpedo-boats and submarines; although he did doubt if any minister would advocate such a policy because of the inevitability of reprisals against French ports.[29]

Naturally such doctrines aroused alarm in a Britain increasingly aware of her vulnerability to all-out naval war against her sea-borne trade. The theme was repeatedly taken up in the papers and discussions of the Royal United Service Institution after 1882 and the casting aside of all restraints was frequently prophesied. Prominent among the speakers was W. G. Crutchley, a master mariner, who was to become secretary of the Navy League:

I'm afraid that modern warfare will probably eclipse in its rigour anything the world has yet seen, and in the endeavour of an enemy to damage the commerce of England, no consideration of ruth or humanity will be entered into ... I think that ships would be sunk promiscuously whenever and wherever they were found, and that this would be carried out even by humane officers, as necessitated by the needs of war.[30]

This was in 1889. In 1893 Crutchley was to issue further warnings about the likelihood of ruthless use of the torpedo. In ironic contrast to this early prophetic realism was the contribution of Captain Prince Louis of Battenberg, destined to be First Sea Lord in 1914, to the subsequent discussion: 'The more I think of it, the more difficulty I have in believing that a civilised Power in the nineteenth century would deliberately sanction its armed forces committing wholesale murder on the high seas.'[31]

The Rejection of Restraint in the First World War

In addition to the theories of the *Jeune École* there were practical factors paving the way towards unrestricted submarine warfare. They originated in the difficulties often encountered by surface warships in carrying out the recognized right of belligerents to visit and search merchantmen on the high seas. It had long been accepted that when circumstances such as weather, the state of the prize or the presence of enemy warships made it dangerous to take her into port for adjudication by a prize court, she could be sunk, after provision had been made for the safety of her passengers and crew. This applied only to enemy merchantmen; neutrals could not be sunk and must be allowed to go free. It was similarly accepted that if a merchantman refused to stop and submit to search, or if she attacked the intercepting warship, she could be fired on and if necessary sunk.[32]

It was of course these restraints on the treatment of passengers and crews and of neutral shipping which Germany rejected during the First World War. She sought to justify her actions by appealing to other traditional rules of international law. They were justified, she claimed, as reprisals against the sufferings inflicted upon her civilian population by the British blockade. Merchantmen lost non-combatant status by being armed and by sending radio intelligence. Neutrals compromised their neutrality by accepting British protection or sailing directions. But there were more cogent reasons. The submarine, operating on the surface, as she would have to do to carry out the traditional practice of visit and search was extremely vulnerable to counter-attack. Furthermore Germany's position by the end of 1916 was so desperate that she saw the efficient use of the submarine as the only possible way of avoiding defeat, and that meant sinking merchantmen without warning.

Between the Wars[33]

Here the main demands for restraint were to come from a Britain clearly aware of how near to defeat she had been in 1917 by unrestricted submarine warfare. In all the naval arms-limitation conferences from Washington onwards she pressed for the abolition of the submarine. This was not acceptable to the other naval powers. France was particularly opposed to it as she saw the submarine as an essential weapon for weaker naval powers. As a substitute, Britain had to follow the lead of the United States in pressing for a code of restrictions on submarine operations in any future war. These restrictions were first formulated in the Root Resolutions of the Washington Conference, expanded in the London Conference of 1930 and made even more stringent by the London Submarine Protocol of 1936. The latter was initially ratified by Britain, the United States, Japan, France and Italy; Germany and the U.S.S.R. acceded later, and by 1939, forty states in all had accepted it.

The cumulative effect of these restraints was to impose on the submarine the same limitations on its conduct towards merchant shipping as those applying to surface warships. Merchantmen must be stopped and visited. They were not to be attacked unless they refused to halt after being warned. They were not to be sunk unless provision had been made for the safety of their passengers and crews; their being allowed to take to the ship's boats was not in itself adequate provision. In passing it should be said that in both world wars German surface raiders did generally keep to these rules. They were included in the German Prize Regulations of 1939 under which both submarine and surface vessels entered the war.

But much more rapidly than in the earlier conflict they were cast aside and replaced by virtually unrestricted submarine warfare.

The Rejection of Restraint in the Second World War

Again Germany produced the legal justification of reprisals, but the fundamental reasons for the rejection of restraints lay in the nature of the war. Once aerial bombardment and invasion had failed, Germany saw the submarine as her only effective weapon against England, and England's defeat was a condition of German survival. Moreover, technical change since 1918 had made the surfaced submarine increasingly vulnerable. More effective locating devices and anti-submarine weapons and, above all, effective maritime aircraft, made it virtually suicidal for submarines to spend the long period on the surface that the process of visit and search demanded. It was these technical factors which were held to justify Allied submarines, in both the European and Pacific theatres, attacking enemy merchantmen without warning – an argument which was successfully used in the defence of Admirals Raeder and Doenitz at Nuremberg.[34]

Conclusion

It would appear that states were willing to accept only such limitations as favoured their own perceived interests, and that when technical development put weapons-systems into their hand which promised success only if used without restriction, then all restraints were cast aside. Machiavelli had said long before:

When the entire safety of our country is at stake no consideration of what is just or unjust, merciful or cruel, praiseworthy or blameworthy must intervene. On the contrary, every other consideration being set aside, that course alone must be taken which preserves the existence of the country and maintains its freedom.[35]

Or, referring more directly to the subject as Admiral Sir John Fisher put it in his inimitable style during the 1899 Hague Peace Conference:

The humanising of war! You might as well talk of humanising hell![36]

NOTES

1. L. Oppenheim, *International Law: A Treatise*, 5th edn., 2 vols., ed. H. Lauterpacht (London, 1935, 1937), II, pp. 189–221, 398–404; G. Schwarzenberger, *A Manual of International Law* (London, 1947), pp. 82–5.
2. Samuel Pepys, *Diary*, 2 Feb. 1664.
3. Michael Howard, *War in European History* (Oxford, 1976), pp. 90–1.
4. Ibid., pp. 97–114.
5. For an introduction to Mahan and Corbett see D. M. Schurman, *The Education of a Navy* (London, 1965), chaps. 4, 7.
6. Julian S. Corbett, *Some Principles of Maritime Strategy* (London, 1911), p. 91.
7. Ibid., pp. 91–6.
8. Oppenheim, op. cit. pp. 358–410, gives a good introduction to the subject.
9. Carlton Savage, *Policy of the United States towards Maritime Commerce in War*, vol. I, 1776–1914 (Washington, 1934; Kraus Reprint, New York, 1969) should be consulted for the evolution of American views.
10. F. T. Piggott, *The Declaration of Paris, 1856* (London, 1919) gives a full account of the negotiations.
11. Savage, op. cit., pp. 68–79, 382–3.
12. W. H. Hall, *International Law*, 3rd edn. (London, 1889), pp. 444–5 outlines Prussian policy in 1866 and 1870.
13. Quoted in Sir Herbert Richmond, *Statesmen and Sea Power* (Oxford, 1946), p. 296.
14. Savage, op. cit., pp. 12–13, 168.
15. Ibid., pp. 46–55.
16. Ibid., p. 391.
17. Ibid., p. 101.
18. Ibid., pp. 103–11.
19. Arthur J. Marder, *From the Dreadnought to Scapa Flow*, vol. 1 (London, 1961), pp. 378–81.
20. Lord Hankey, *The Supreme Command 1914–1918*, vol. 1 (London, 1961), pp. 94–101.
21. Oppenheim, op. cit., pp. 625–55, 655–88, gives a full analysis of blockade and contraband. Savage, op. cit., vol. II, pp. 163–79, gives the full text of the Declaration.
22. Hankey, op. cit., pp. 94–5.
23. Ibid., p. 355; Savage, op. cit., vol. II, p. 3.
24. W. Arnold Foster, *The New Freedom of the Seas* (London, 1942), chaps. 5–10 gives an interesting analysis of the relationship between the Declaration of London and what actually happened in war. S. W. Roskill, *Naval Policy between the Wars*, vol. 1 (London, 1968), pp. 80–2, summarizes Anglo–American differences on "The Freedom of the Seas".

25. Savage, op. cit., vol. II, pp. 11–14, 18, 34, 40–1, 267–8.
26. Arthur J. Marder, *The Anatomy of British Sea Power* (London, 1964), chap. VI, analyses the thought and influence of the *Jeune École* and the British reaction.
27. Gabriel Charmes, *La Réforme de la marine* (Paris, 1886); English trans., *Naval Reform*, by J. E. Gordon Cummings (London, 1887), pp. 61–2, 71, 79–80.
28. Commandants 'Z', et H. Montéchant, *Essai de stratégie navale*, Paris and Nancy, 1893, pp. ix–xvii, 19–26, 64–6.
29. J. L. de Lanessan, *La Programme maritime de 1900–1906* (Paris, 1903). There is an approved translation in *RUSI Journal*, vol. XLVII (1903), pp. 1024 ff.
30. W. G. Crutchley, 'On the Unprotected State of British Commerce at Sea', *RUSI Journal*, vol. XXXIII (1889–1900), p. 630.
31. W. G. Crutchley, 'Modern Warfare as Affecting the Mercantile Marine of Great Britain', *RUSI Journal*, vol. XXXVII (1893), pp. 494, 506–7.
32. Oppenheim, op. cit., pp. 370–3, 389–92.
33. Extensive coverage of the subject can be found in: H. and M. Sprout, *Towards a New Order of Sea Power* (New York, 1940, reprinted 1969), pp. 190–216 and in S. W. Roskill, op. cit., vol. I, chaps. VIII, XIV, vol. II (1976), chaps. II, X.
34. Grand Admiral Raeder, *Struggle for the Sea* (London, 1959), pp. 248–9; Admiral Doenitz, *Memoirs* (London, 1959), pp. 58–9.
35. Quoted in Hankey, op. cit., p. 352. A slightly differing version in Machiavelli, *Discourses*, ed. B. Crick (London, 1970), p. 515.
36. Quoted in Admiral Sir R. H. Bacon, *The Life of Lord Fisher of Kilverstone* (London, 1929), vol. I, p. 121.

4

RESTRAINTS ON WAR IN THE AIR BEFORE 1945

Donald Cameron Watt

Like the majority of those living in Britain today, I was too young to see military service in 1939–45. Unlike most of today's university population, I *was* called up, to do military service, soon after my eighteenth birthday in 1946. Ten months later I found myself on a troop train proceeding slowly through northern France and southern Germany towards the British occupied zone of Southern Austria. My wartime adolescence was spent near Coventry; and I had paid brief visits to London while it was under bombardment by V2s. The Austria to which I was going had largely, save for Vienna, escaped the fighting and the bombing. But the landscape through which the troop train passed was quite another matter. Although it was two years since the German surrender, the train still crossed the rivers which cut through southern Germany by Bailey bridges. The towns through which one passed were at best in ruins, at worst mounds of weed-strewn rubble through which streets had been driven. One town, Pforzheim, had, so far as we could see, not a single roof standing. Later the extent of the catastrophe which overtook Europe's heritage of art and architecture was to become more apparent. I recall in 1968 walking through the middle of Frankfurt where the medieval town stood, and which was still largely flat and bare. It was in the same year that the gaps torn by German bombers aiming at Euston and King's Cross, in the Georgian square in Bloomsbury where I live were finally filled and the great classical façade restored to its original shape. Yet by contrast with the real disasters, Warsaw, Rotterdam, London's City churches, Belgrade, Hamburg, Dresden, not to speak of Tokyo, Hiroshima, and Nagasaki, what I myself have seen are merely footnotes to the orgy of artistic and aesthetic self-impoverishment inflicted on itself between 1939 and 1945 by the warring world. And many would add, the aesthetic losses pale before the cost in life, limb, and human misery to which they were the accompaniment.

A very substantial part of this destruction was wrought by attack from the air. With the single exception of Warsaw, most of these cities I have so far mentioned were not directly fought over. Berlin, Budapest, Caen, Leningrad, Odessa, and many other cities in Russia were fought over, often at short range and the destruction was comparably great. But as much or even more of the destruction caused during the war years came from bombing from the air, bombing which in many cases was designed not to remove military targets but to destroy civilian morale. In recent celebrations of the late Lord Avon's public career, no one recalled that it was he who suggested that since 'the psychological effects of bombing have little connexion with the military or economic importance of the target', being 'determined solely by the amount of destruction and dislocation caused ... the claims of smaller towns of under 150,000 inhabitants, which are not too heavily defended, should be considered even though those towns contain only targets of secondary importance',[1] a curious index of how war to defend civilization can destroy its spirit even among those who lead its defence. Since 1945, still more since the advent of the H-bomb and the ballistic missile, we have all lived in the shadow of still greater holocausts of fire, heat, and radiation capable of devastating and rendering areas several counties wide into wildernesses for generations. In this context to look at the efforts made in the first forty years of this century to inhibit, limit, and control the use of air power in modern warfare can only be profoundly depressing – depressing, but none the less instructive.

Instruction comes in various packages. In the case of the subject under discussion, there are three particular and individual aspects which make it of special interest. The first is the attempt of an advanced but still belligerent society to devise restraints and inhibitions on the use of a weapon the technological development of which was so constantly to be out of phase with men's concepts of its use. The second is the manner in which those concerned with the problem moved from optimism to extreme pessimism in their attitudes to the weapon and the technology that produced it. The third is the decline of overall moral standards and the dwindling of the ethical horizons of those responsible from a general to a purely national scale.

To take these in order: the idea of regulating and limiting the activity of warfare by establishing agreed rules is an aspect of the whole drive of late nineteenth-century Europe towards establishing and codifying the ground rules of an emergent pan-European, transnational society. It goes *pari passu* with the intermarrying of Europe's crowned heads and to a lesser extent its aristocracy and grand bourgeoisie; with the development of institutions of co-operation in the political and economic fields such as ambassadors' conferences and banking consortia; with the growth of the international regulation of posts, telegraphs, and cables; with the emergence of the international congresses of scientists, historians, and athletes.[2] When that society was largely destroyed in the first round of the European civil war, that which raged between 1914 and 1918, it re-emerged as part of the substitution of a written constitution, the Covenant of the League of Nations, for the *ad hoc* growth of customary law prior to 1914, where the main effort is put not into establishing laws of war but in limiting the weapons with which war is fought. When that in turn broke down in 1933 there was a revival of interest in the idea of establishing rules and conventions of war based on an imagined common interest between belligerents which, while it held good for chemical and biological warfare, was hopeless from the beginning where the dropping of explosive bombs was concerned.

The first attempt to obtain international agreement over the dropping of explosives from the air took place at the first Hague Conference in 1899. The original draft Russian proposals contained a clause prohibiting the discharge of projectiles or explosives of any kind from balloons or by similar methods. At that date, though men had dreamed of flight for centuries, the only practicable flying machines were free, non-dirigible balloons, which had been in use for 115 years. In 1812 the Russians had attempted to use a balloon filled with explosives against Napoleon during his advance on

Moscow. In 1849 the Austrians had tried to bomb Venice by similar means. Both attempts had failed. Thereafter the balloon, free or captive, had been regularly used in war for observation work, but nothing more. The Russian delegate at the Hague spoke of experiments with man-carrying kites. General den Baer Portugael of the Netherlands spoke of the use of balloons to drop poisonous gases from the air. Russia's own efforts to construct a dirigible airship had just ended in disaster but she was uncomfortably aware that where she had failed, French and German programmes designed to produce lighter-than-air power-driven dirigibles were on the verge of success. Two international conferences, one in Chicago in 1893 and one in Paris also in 1899, had discussed the possible use of dirigible airships in war. Count Zeppelin made his first flight in 1900 a few months after the Hague Conference had disbanded. Within seven years he had a vehicle capable of carrying 1,400 kilograms for 12 hours for a striking range of 150 miles.[3]

The delegates to the Hague were, in fact, well aware that the conquest of the air was imminent. How far the first instruments of that conquest could be used in war was a very different matter. While delegates from the smaller nations and from the more backward argued for an absolute prohibition, those from America, Britain, France, and Germany strongly opposed them. It was the American delegate, Captain Crozier, whose Board of Ordnance had put $50,000 into Mr. Langley's attempt to scale up his model steam aeroplane, which had actually flown, into a heavier-than-air life-size 'aerodrome', who proposed as a compromise that the prohibition should run five years only. The British remained opposed in principle even to so limited a compromise, but abandoned their opposition in return for American support in their resistance to the condemnation of dum-dum bullets.[4] Where some delegates struck what we would now call Doomwatch attitudes, Lord Wolseley, then Commander-in-Chief of the British Army, was forthright in his views. Dropping bombs from balloons would, if it proved possible, confer an enormous advantage on a power like Britain which possessed only a small army. 'In war superior armament compensates for lack of numerical strength.' Further –

Restrictions on scientific inventions deprive a nation of the advantages which accrue from its scientific men and from the productive capacity of its manufacturing establishments.

It can be proved to the hilt that scientific development of engines of destruction had tended

(a) to make nations hesitate before going to war;
(b) to reduce the percentages of losses in war;
(c) to shorten the lengths of campaigns, and thus to reduce to a minimum the sufferings endured by the inhabitants.[5]

Three years later, the Wright brothers lifted their plane off the soil of the United States. While Germany concentrated on the Zeppelin, France led the way with the heavier-than-air craft. When the Second Hague Conference met in 1907, France, Germany, Russia, and Italy had already embarked on the substantial production of military dirigibles. Only Britain and the United States, where the Wright brothers' flight was an isolated incident not followed by the explosion of activity which followed their demonstration three years later in France and Italy, remained untouched. Both therefore supported a renewal of the five year prohibition, the British delegate Lord Reay demanding indefinite prohibition until a third conference should be able to settle the matter. For Lord Reay, competition on land and at sea was quite enough of a burden on national finance without adding a similar burden on the budget to maintain an adequate air force. Lord Reay alone was not enough to withstand the march of progress, dramatically underlined by the arrival of the Franco–Brazilian pioneer of the air Santos-Dumont in his plane for the closing of the conference.[6] The restriction on air bombardment was rescinded. Four years later, during the Italian war on Turkey of 1911–12, the first bombs were dropped from the air in war by Italian aircraft operating in Libya. The targets were Arab villagers.[7]

As so often actuality was far behind the imaginations of literature. The rapid spiral of technological development beginning in the 1870s with the invention of the internal combustion engine coincided with the development of the military fiction-writer to produce a school of science-fiction writers imitating Jules Verne and H. G. Wells. While thriller writers, such as Erskine Childers, and political tract writers and humanists dealt in their various ways with a future

German invasion of Britain, General Swinton, masquerading under the dreadful pen-name of Ole Luke-Oie, was writing of one-man flyers destroying vital river bridges to trap a retreating army or ramming one another in the sky to prevent the defencelessness of their own infantry's positions being discovered.[8] And H. G. Wells's imagination was leaping on; the vision of airborne atomic warfare in Europe, *The War in the Air*, was published six years before the outbreak of war in 1914.[9]

The bitterness of the belligerents, their frustration and their consequent reliance on frightfulness in the years 1914–18, were soon to prove the essential frailty of the movement to limit and restrain war by agreed rules. Even the rules on prisoners of war and internees proved impossible to uphold in the chaos of the collapse of the Russian front in 1917. Poison-gas, reprisals against civilians, unrestricted submarine warfare, and unrestricted blockade at sea made a nonsense of the laws of war. In the air the exigencies of war took aeronautics in four short years from the short-ranged butterflies of 1914 to the giant Handley-Page four-engined bombers of 1918, capable of crossing the Atlantic, whereas Blériot had only just made it across the Channel ten years earlier. German aircraft and airships bombed England and France, concentrating mainly on London and south-east England. The raids of 1917 led directly, under the influence of Major-General Trenchard upon General Smuts, to the establishment of the Royal Air Force upon the amalgamation of the Royal Flying Corps and the Royal Naval Air Service, and to the establishment in October 1917 in France of the Independent Bombing Force to carry the strategic bombing offensive to the German people. Raids into the Saarland and towards Mannheim and Stuttgart did a certain amount of destruction and killed a certain number of civilians. They seem also to have provoked the last dying effort of those who hoped agreements might be reached to restrain the belligerents.

The initiative came from the King of Spain who, so the Spanish ambassador in London reported, had been in communication with the German Government with a view to getting some check put on the bombing of undefended towns.[10]

The Cabinet agreed to consider this; there then followed a statement in the Bavarian parliament which appeared to signify a German willingness to abandon air attack on open towns if the Allies would do the same. The Cabinet considered this offer, fortified by a General Staff memorandum pointing out that with trench lines stretching from Switzerland to the sea, in some sense every German town was defended. They concluded that any limitation of bombing to the battlefield areas within reach of the front line would add to the hazards suffered by the population of occupied northern France and of Belgium; whereas it was 'undesirable in the interests of future peace that the civilian population of Germany should be the one population among the belligerents to enjoy immunity'. Britain in short would not accept any limitations on her freedom to develop what Lord Weir, the new Air Minister, described in a memo to the Cabinet as a 'rapid development of aerial forces devoted to the interruption of German industrial effort and kindred objectives'.

During the whole inter-war period, the statesmen and diplomatists were to attempt to restrain the scope of war in the air by three different approaches: the limitation of air forces in the quantity and quality of the aircraft at their disposal; the prohibition of certain forms of weapon and warfare; and the establishment of international rules for that weapon. Each had its peculiar difficulties. Limitation by quantity and quality raised three kinds of questions: the first had to do with the limits established and the ratios of strength permitted to each power; the second had to do with the possible use of civilian forms of the weapon and their conversion to military purposes during war, from the riot policemen turned paramilitary infantrymen to the fast merchant ship with its six-inch guns, mine-laying equipment, and torpedo tubes; the third arose because any proposal embodied of necessity an attempt to stop the clock, to put a halt on technological development which had its own entirely non-military impetus. The second approach, the prohibition of certain forms of weapon, again raised the problem of the conversion of civilian forms of weapon in wartime. It may be difficult to imagine why any power should want more than a small number of short range submersibles in peace. But civilian air transport could readily be adapted for use as bombing aircraft. Indeed the German Junkers Ju 52, a three-engined transport of the 1930s, was designed so that the minimum of retooling could set the same production lines to turning out a bomber. As for the third, it raised again the much vexed question of enforcement. Who, if anyone, could ensure more than a lingering shadow existence for any rules of war agreed in peace once war had begun?

The easiest form of international restriction to achieve is that imposed by the victor upon the vanquished. The victors in the 1914–18 war could stop the clock for Germany; or at least they did their utmost. By Article 198 of the Treaty of Versailles Germany was forbidden to possess a military or naval air force, and the construction of new military aircraft was prohibited. Article 201 forbade all manufacturing of aircraft or their importation for six months, a prohibition that was not lifted until 1922. Article 202 provided for the delivery of the Allies of all aeronautical equipment (and its destruction). When the prohibition included in Article 201 was lifted, the Council of Ambassadors, at the instance of the French, laid down severe restrictions on the size, engine power, fuel capacity, and flying speed permissible to German civil aviation. At the same time France rapidly built up the air forces of her new eastern allies, while her own air force was built up to 152 squadrons with a huge reserve, of which just under half were organized into bombardment groups.

The example of France was followed by Italy, especially after Mussolini's advent to power, where a target of 100 squadrons was aimed at by 1925. A powerful aircraft industry was built up, and about half the air force was organized for bombing attack. Britain by contrast cut her wartime strength to 21 squadrons. Alarm at the size of the French air force, half of which was deployed around Paris, led in 1923 to the establishment of a target of 52 squadrons. The R.A.F. survived efforts to break it down into its component military and naval co-operation sections after it had been able to demonstrate in Somalia, against 'the Mad Mullah', and in Iraq, its effectiveness as a cheap means of controlling wild tribesmen in terrain which gave them the advantage over civilized infantry. It went on to develop a doctrine of the strategic bombing offensive pure and unadulterated as the new, indeed the only, way of waging war in the era of technology.

As a doctrine, this appealed to the instinctive feeling of the elder statesmen, who were called on to pronounce upon it, that they were living in an age of technological revolution. This doctrine was, of course, only in a limited sense the product of technologists or aimed at them. Despite Lord Trenchard's hopes of money for research, not even the simplest surveys were made of the lessons of the bombing of the 1914–18 war or of the additional technological developments in airframe construction, bomb sights, navigation aids and so on necessary to translate his crudely argued and roughly muttered *obiter dicta* into reality. He made his greatest impact on the metaphysicians, Smuts and Balfour. No real technical progress was made by the R.A.F. under him, and it was not until his retirement that the assembled abilities of the British scientific community were turned to the service of air warfare and the 'boffin' was born. When one thinks what a handful of enthusiasts did to keep Britain's tanks alive in the same period, Lord Trenchard's tenure of the post of Chief of Air Staff seems even more peculiar. What he did do, of course, was to create not an air force but a new armed service with its own deep-rooted loyalties, courage and *esprit-de-corps*. What he also did was to promulgate within the machinery of government a fear of air warfare and of Britain's particular vulnerability to air attack which became an obstacle even to the efficient functioning of the Air Force and of the policy he advocated. In terms of our analysis he remained almost alone among the senior echelons of British Government as the spokesman of optimism. Technological development had, he insisted, provided a deterrent against war, and a way of fighting it quickly and cheaply. Megatechnology of the naval kind was a thing of the past – so were the vast armies of 1916–18. The bombing offensive would strike to the heart of an enemy's war-making capacity.[11]

Trenchard's theorizing found little hearing outside government. For the rest of the world thoughts of disarmament were

dominant. The Washington Conference of 1922, now remem-
bered simply as an instrument of naval limitation, was
intended to cover all armaments. Its sub-committee on aircraft
was the first of a succession of international gatherings to
grapple with the question of how far it was possible to impose
limitations on aircraft, either military or civil.[12] It decided
that limitation of a country's commercial aeronautics could
only be imposed as a deliberate move to limit the military air
power of a state and thus avoid war. The reverse of the coin
of course was that commercial aeronautics as such could not
be controlled. The question of limiting military aircraft ran at
once into the problem of comparability between the very
different ways the air strength of a country could be calculated,
and the impossibility of fixing ratios was noted. The sub-
committee, indeed, concluded flatly that the limitation of
military aircraft was not practicable. The attention of the
Conference turned therefore to the question of laws of war.
Here it ran into the flat refusal of the European powers, who
had come to Washington quite unprepared for this kind of
thing, to discuss the U.S. draft: they were prepared however
to accept a resolution setting up a Commission to consider
whether the existing rules of international law covered 'new
methods of attack or defense resulting from the introduction
since the Hague Conference of 1907 of new agencies of
warfare' – and if they did not, what to do about it.[13]

This Commission of jurists succeeded in obtaining agreement on a number of rules of war in the air. The most vital
were those dealing with the much vexed question of military
and civilian targets. Article 22 of the General Report
specifically forbade attack from the air for the purpose of
terrorizing the civil population or of injuring non-combatants.
Article 23 proclaimed bombing to be legitimate only when
directed at a military target defined as one whose destruction
would constitute a distinct military advantage. It prohibited
bombing of cities, towns, and villages not in the immediate
neighbourhood of operations on the ground. Moreover where
bombing targets were so situated that they could not be
bombarded without the indiscriminate bombing of the civilian
population, then there was to be no bombing at all.[14]

Britain co-operated in all this, though the Air Ministry was properly contemptuous. But their civilian lords and masters had in November 1921 discovered the 'continental air menace'; throughout 1922 the C.I.D. discussed the issue through various committees.[15] The outcome was the 52 squadron programme of 1923. And while Sir Hugh Trenchard spread alarm and despondency through the Cabinet and the corridors of Whitehall with his apocalyptic pictures of a new World War opening with an all-out air attack on London, a quarter of a million casualties, riots and disorder on a scale which would necessitate military intervention, the Foreign Office had to cope with the preparatory Committee for the World Disarmament Conference, which met in various sub-committees including one on the air. On that committee the British role was consistently to urge the drastic limitation of aerial armaments and the abolition of bombing from the air. Lord Wolseley's optimism had given way to fear. Britain was vulnerable: Britain was no longer an island, and while the air staff fought for the retention of some bombing capacity for police purposes in the remoter parts of empire, thinking in the Foreign Office and on the Cabinet Committee on disarmament turned steadily towards the limitation of air forces and the prohibition of bombing from the air.

The World Disarmament Conference met in Geneva in February 1932 after seven years of preparations. Its assemblage represented the peak point of the League of Nations' efforts to expand its field of activity until it was genuinely a world as well as a European security organization. Both the great outsiders, the future Superpowers, America and Russia, were to take an active part on its deliberations. Throughout the 1920s despite the hypocrisy, the manœuvring for national advantage, the mushroom growth of international bureaucracy and the endless windy rhetoric so admirably satirized in *Clochemerle, England Their England* and elsewhere, the League and the preparatory commission for the disarmament conference had moved the major powers steadily towards the conference table and towards the idea of collaboration and argument rather than isolation and conflict. Much of the underpinning of this movement had been gradually eroded

since 1926, especially since the Wall Street crash of 1929 and
the events of the terrible year,[16] as Arnold Toynbee called it,
of 1931. It is difficult even now, even conscious as the historian
must be of the endless archives of finally futile quasi-
metaphysical argument about the relative merits of this or
that solution to this or that question, to avoid the image of a
meeting at sea in which those present reach out their hands to
one another ever more desperately as their individual craft
are swept inexorably apart.

In essence the disarmament conference can be seen as an
occasion where four to five separate policies met and clashed.
The French, with their rotten-borough support from the
Little-Entente countries, wanted to perpetuate the military
status quo. In this aim they had involved themselves in
gratuitous conflict with Fascist Italy, gratuitous since the
conflict had nothing to do with their overall aim but resulted
from their attachment to the idea of hierarchies of powers,
such as that established by the Washington Naval Treaty.
The British wanted desperately to cling to a *status quo* which
threatened at any moment to dissolve into an arms race they
no longer had the confidence that they could lead. The
Russian aim was to prevent the coalition of her capitalist
enemies into an anti-Soviet league and to exploit all
opportunities to enlist the public opinions of her enemies
against their governments and towards the Soviet Union as
the spearhead of the movement for world peace. The Germans
wanted freedom from the restriction of Versailles or the
disarming of other states of their level. More than that, the
German Government, without a parliamentary majority, and
increasingly unable to control the war in the streets between
Nazi and Communist, wanted a public success. The Italians
wanted parity with France. The American Secretary of State,
Henry Stimson, and the U.S. East-Coast establishment, wanted
a success and one which would acknowledge U.S. leadership.
In the air this led the French to press outright for the putting
of all aircraft, civil and bombing, under League control with
only short-range fighters remaining with the national air
forces. The League was to have the only force of long-range
heavy bombers permitted.

With this the French had broached the whole complex of questions bound up with quantitative and qualitative disarmament, aggressive and defensive weapons, the position of reserves in the calculation of forces and so on. The conference itself went through various phases. The first saw the publication of rival plans. The second concerned itself almost exclusively with the problem of German equality of rights. President Hoover then threw a new U.S. plan into the conference like a heavy stone splashing into a pond. With that the conference went into recess until suddenly in December 1932 a formula emerged which satisfied for the time being the German position on equality of rights. When the smoke cleared away it was clear the initiative had passed exclusively to Britain. Sir John Simon had already put a British plan in reply to President Hoover. Now, in March 1933, Ramsay MacDonald put forward a new British plan, essentially an interim solution. But time was running out. Hitler had come to power in January. In October he took Germany out of both League and Disarmament Conference. It lasted another six months and then adjourned *sine die*.

The Conference came close to virtual unanimity at two levels on the issues of war in the air. At the technical level the Air Commission reporting in June 1932 made it plain once again that all air armaments could be used offensively and that civil aircraft could to varying degrees be subsumed into military ends.[17] The sole promising line to pursue was, they thought, the limitation of the size of construction, the load carryable, and the range of operation. At the political level only Britain stood out against the total abolition of bombing aircraft and bombing from the air, since the Air Ministry insisted, against the bitter opposition of the Foreign Office, on retaining bombers for police purposes in the remoter parts of empire. At the General Commission on 22 May 1933 Britain found this reservation denounced by all but the delegates from Iraq, Iran, and Thailand – not the most reputable of allies. The roasting that ministers suffered in the British press and in parliament was even more embarrassing. Anthony Eden was driven to say that the British reservation in favour of the use of bombing planes for purposes of policing unruly tribesmen could and would be abandoned if the Conference seemed likely to fail on this issue.[18] By then however the moment, if there ever was a moment, had passed. In October 1933 Hitler withdrew Germany from both League and Disarmament Conference.

From 1933 to 1936 Britain and France devoted themselves to attempts to manœuvre Germany back into the circle of international discussion. Successive French cabinets, anxious as ever for France's security, preferred to attempt to organize international alignments with Italy and the Soviet Union, with the aim of so boxing Hitler in that acceptance of French terms was the only alternative to continuing and frustrating isolation. The British Government, deeply conscious of Britain's overall military weakness and sensitive to the point of obsession with Britain's vulnerability to air attack, preferred to treat directly with Germany on a basis of trading off legitimization of Hitler's presumed objectives in return for his willingness to enter again on international discussions aimed at agreement on arms limitation and general pacification. At all costs an outright confrontation had to be avoided until Britain's rearmament had reached a level where it could be expected to play an important role in Hitler's own calculations. The French policy reflected the native bellicosity of spirit of M. Barthou, the French Foreign Minister, who originated it. It was to run into the sands as first Hitler's proclamation of German rearmament in March 1935, then the Italian conflict with the League over Abyssinia, and finally the German remilitarization of the Rhineland in March 1936 revealed its fatal weakness, the absence of any coercive element in it. French cabinets between 1933 and 1938 appear to have devoted little thought and less understanding to the role of force in international affairs. The British Cabinet, by contrast, was dominated by calculations of military strength, to the exclusion almost of any other argument, whether of honour or credibility. Both were to come together briefly in 1935 in a proposal to conclude an Air Pact to reinforce their mutual security.

The main aims of British policy in this regard – and one should note that the other major actors in the 1932–3

Disarmament Conference, Russia, America, and Italy, evinced no interest in the matter whatever: discussion was confined entirely to Britain, France and Germany – the main British aims, I say, were to secure an international agreement to limit the levels of strengths of the major air forces and to secure an international agreement against air bombardment. The proposal for an air pact to supplement the provisions of the Treaty of Locarno on the ground came from the French in peculiar and still unexplained circumstances in February 1935 when M. Flandin and M. Laval visited London. The French ministers had given no prior indication that they intended to advance such a proposal until two or three days before the visit.[19] It is entirely possible that the idea was a last-minute reaction to hints from the British side that this was one area in which Britain might be able to make a gesture towards the constant French demand for more security: the essential element on the French side being their demand that it be backed by staff talks. For the French it was to be just one element in a mesh of new Locarno-style security pacts, on Germany's eastern frontier, in the Danubian area and so on, in which Hitler's ambitions were to be trapped. For the British the important element was their desire that it might form the basis for the agreement on limitation of forces in the air towards which their hopes were directed, and which was to be traded off first for a legitimization of Hitler's clandestine rearmament, then for the acceptance of the remilitarization of the Rhineland.[20]

In the background to these discussions Treasury, Foreign Office, War Office, and Admiralty were embroiled in a bitter battle with the Air Ministry over the direction of British rearmament in the air. True to their faith in the gospel according to Trenchard the Air Staff insisted that the only protection against bombers was the deterrent effect of having more and bigger bombers, massive retaliation, the strategic offensive. It was in 1935 that the Air Ministry made the first moves towards acquiring the massive force of four-engined heavy bombers on which the wartime strategic air offensive was to be based. The Treasury felt that the major thrust of the rearmament effort should go into the creation of an air defence for Great Britain, searchlights, anti-aircraft guns, fighter squadrons and the 'boffins'' providential discovery, radio-location. Desire to recover some of the financial support given to this programme could be relied on to make the War Office and Admiralty support any proposals that might be advanced for an international agreement to limit the use of bombing in war. But just as the successive shocks of 1935–6 brought the initiatives of MM. Barthou and Laval to nought, so the uncanny knack Hitler had of seizing unilaterally what the British were just about to offer him as trade goods made the British policy seem equally pointless. The end came with the long-drawn-out and entirely abortive efforts of Mr. Anthony Eden (as he then was) to conclude a new security pact in the west to replace Locarno.[21]

In 1936 therefore there began to manifest itself in the inner discussions of the Chiefs of Staff and the Committee of Imperial Defence a renewed interest in an international convention on the rules of air warfare.[22] This interest ran into a good deal of scepticism, but it was to keep itself alive until February 1939, when, like so much else of pre-war strategic debate, it was a casualty of that sudden conversion of Cabinet and defence staff to the imminence of war with Germany which popular historical writing still ascribes to the reaction to Hitler's breach of the Munich Agreement in March 1939, but as is now clear was a product of the Cabinet's reaction to the war-scare of mid-January 1939.

This interest was reinforced by the pressure of public anxieties. Since the late 1920s the official fear of a knock-out air attack on London in the initial stages of a war, if indeed it was not the substitute for a formal declaration of war, had been echoed in public by a series of books on the shape of war to come comparable in their scope to the invasion scare literature before 1914. From 1936 onwards any public apprehension that this literature either raised or reflected was enormously enhanced by the newsreel shots of the effects of air bombardment in the Spanish Civil War. There were no news cameras at Guernica, only reporters of differing biases. But the bombing of Barcelona could be seen in weekly instalments. The Non-Intervention Committee indeed in June 1937 called on both sides to abstain from the destruction of open towns and villages and other objectives of a non-military character;[23] but they called in vain.

In November 1937 Lord Halifax paid his famous visit to Germany in the disguise of a Master of Foxhounds. In conversation with him Hitler who was, believe it or not, an opponent of blood sports, touched upon the possibility of negotiations looking towards agreed restrictions on the use of bombing in war.[24] In British circles it was believed that while London was the most vulnerable target in Europe, the Ruhr came a close second and that Hitler had reason to be apprehensive at the effect on critical sections of the German war economy of French air attack on its cities and industries. These beliefs were given a further fillip by a conversation between von Ribbentrop and Sir Neville Henderson in February 1938;[25] but a speech Hitler made in the Reichstag a fortnight later and a change in Ribbentrop's own attitude a week after that put paid to such hopes.[26]

British discussion however revived in June 1938.[27] A contributing factor must have been the discovery that fear of German air attack on Paris was overwhelming French thinking. But the central factor was undoubtedly the Air Ministry's belated discovery that the Royal Air Force was in no position to strike, pre-emptively or retaliatorily, against German air bases and that the whole basis of British air policy was destroyed.[28] Discussions in the Sub-Committee of the C.I.D. accepted that any agreement on the limitation of bombing in wartime could only be of a short duration. Nevertheless it would still be in Britain's interests as it would make an enemy 'hesitate to take the gloves off'. What is the more surprising is that the Sub-Committee seriously entertained the proposition that to secure such an agreement, with all that it implied for the protection of London and south-east England, Britain should be prepared not only to forgo the chance of damaging the German industries of the Ruhr but also that she should offer not to impose a naval blockade on Germany into the bargain.

This proposal was duly shot down in January 1939 by the Sub-Committee on Warfare and Trade.[29] But the Air Staff continued to argue that nothing should be done which might provoke Germany into a bombing offensive. In October 1938 the directors of planning estimated that Germany could drop 600 tons of bombs a day on Britain to the mere 100 tons per day that Britain and France could drop on Germany.[30] In February 1939 the Chiefs of Staff underlined the argument by stating that it was 'no part of British policy' to initiate air attacks on Germany;[31] this was reiterated in April 1939 by the Strategic Appreciation Sub-Committee.[32] Anglo–French plans, it said, should be based on the assumption that 'we shall not initiate air attacks against any but purely military objectives in the narrowest sense of the term ... and the question whether we are the first to bomb at all must be a matter for decision by the respective Governments at the time'.

In effect this amounted to the unilateral acceptance of the Hague rules. It paved the way towards the final footnote with which this chaper must end – the tacit observance of these rules by all combatants in the West for the first nine months of the war. No such observance occurred in the Polish campaign. President Roosevelt's appeal early in September 1939[33] provided an excuse for both Hitler and Chamberlain to avow their desire not to be the first to unleash unrestricted air warfare on the civilian populations of Europe (Poland always excepted). On the British side the calculations of the planners were reinforced by the grandiose anxieties of the French who, as at Munich, dreamt of their cities in ruins and their air force destroyed, so far had it fallen behind that of Germany in the years the locusts had eaten.

To recapitulate: the history of the efforts to limit, restrain, and inhibit the operations of war in the air shows such efforts to have had one of three alternative aims: the limitation of armaments by quantity and quality; the prohibition of bombing from the air; and the limitation of such bombing to rigidly defined military targets. These efforts took place against the background of a rapidly evolving technology and of reactions to the rate of evolution which only too often, both among the general public and the air staffs of the powers themselves, outstripped the capacities of the moment. Initial reactions to these developments were hopeful and optimistic; but the experience of the 1914–18 war substituted fears of a cataclysm for the hopes of an end to war.

The movement began in the last decade of the world which died in 1914, a world in which transnational ties and a network of conventions amounting in strength to that of customary law created an image and, to a point, a consensus for the nature of international society. After the breakdown of 1914–18, direct efforts were made to rebuild this society on the basis not of customary law but of a written constitution. Efforts to limit the use of this now rapidly advancing means of war took place against a background of a world in which the Superpowers of the future had begun by isolating themselves from the League of Nations but moved towards it though the instrumentality of the Disarmament Conference and its preparatory Committee. This second stage lasted until 1933–4 when Hitler withdrew from the Conference and the French later adjourned the Conference *sine die*; but the society within which the World Disarmament Conference took place was dead before Hitler came to power, perhaps even before the Conference itself met. The third stage was one in which the powers of the *status quo* tried to manœuvre those who wished to destroy it into positions of inactivity, and failed miserably – inevitably but miserably. This last stage was marked by an attempt to return to the limitation of war by convention and law. It failed, but tenderness towards neutral opinion secured that, for the first nine months of the war, the Hague rules were largely observed on the western front. Thereafter Europe slid into that destruction of its own cultural, artistic, architectural, and urban heritage to which I referred fleetingly in my opening remarks. And we are all of us infinitely the poorer.

NOTES

1. Sir Charles Webster and Noble Frankland, *The Strategic Air Offensive against Germany 1939–45* (London, 1961), vol. IV, p. 115.
2. J. F. S. Lyons, *Internationalism in Europe, 1815–1914* (Leyden, 1963), *passim*; D. C. Watt, *Too Serious a Business: European Armed Forces and the Approach of the Second World War* (London and Berkeley, 1975), pp. 16–17.

3. M. W. Royse, *Aerial Bombardment and the International Regulation of Warfare* (New York, 1928), pp. 22–50; J. B. Scott, *The Hague Peace Conferences* (Baltimore, 1909); ibid., *The Proceedings of the Hague Peace Conferences, the Conference of 1899* (New York, 1920).

4. Public Record Office, F.O. 412/65.

5. F.O. 412/65; Wolseley to Secretary of State, 7 Oct. 1899.

6. Royse, op. cit., pp. 59 note 1, 60–1, 97–122. Britain's air forces at this date were described in the House of Commons as consisting of 'one toy airship at Aldershot and one airplane which will not fly'. *Parl. Deb.*, 2 Aug. 1909, col. 1576.

7. Royse, op. cit., p. 211 note 128.

8. Ole Luke-Oie, *The Green Curve Omnibus* (London, 1942). The stories here collected all date from before 1914.

9. H. G. Wells, *The War in the Air* (London, 1908).

10. On this episode see H. A. Jones, *The War in the Air*, vol. VI (London, 1922), pp. 101–6.

11. On the thinking of the British Air Staff in this period see Webster and Frankland, op. cit., vol. I, pp. 55–64; H. Montgomery Hyde, *British Air Policy between the Wars, 1918–1939* (London, 1976), pp. 137–8, 223–8. See also CAB 207, CP 332, Air Staff Memorandum, 'The War Object of an Air Force'.

12. Royse, op. cit., pp. 206–11; *Conference on the Limitation of Armaments, Washington, 1921–22* (Washington, D.C., 1922), pp. 752 ff., for the proceedings and report of the sub-committee.

13. *Report of the Commission of Jurists* (The Hague, 1923); John Bassett Moore, *International Law and Some Current Illusions and other Essays* (New York, 1924), pp. 182 ff.; Royse, op. cit., pp. 211–14, 217–20.

14. Royse, op. cit., pp. 213–14.

15. P.R.O. CAB 3/3.

16. *Survey of International Affairs, 1931* (London, 1932).

17. *Records of the Conference for the Reduction and Limitation of Armaments*, Minutes of the Air Commission (Geneva, 1932–3).

18. *Parl. Deb.*, 5th Series, vol. 279, col. 129; vol. 372; Montgomery Hyde, op. cit., pp. 278–95.

19. To be exact, on 25 Jan. 1935; CAB 21/413; F.O. 371/18825, C962/55/18.

20. F.O. 371/18824, C892/55/18; Uri Bialer, 'Some Aspects of the Fear of Bombardment from the Air and the Making of British Defence and Foreign Policy, 1932–1939', University of London, Ph.D. thesis 1974, pp. 134–69.

21. Bialer, op. cit., pp. 170–82; J. T. Emmerson, *The Rhineland Crisis, 7 March 1936* (London, 1977), pp. 227–35.

22. Bialer, op. cit., pp. 185 ff. CAB 53/6, C.O.S. 181st Meeting 1936; Cab 4/24, C.I.D. 1246.B; CAB 2/6, C.I.D. 1276.B, 28th meeting.

23. P.R.O., F.O. 371/20700, C7862/148/62. See also Hugh Thomas, *The Spanish Civil War* (London, 1914), pp. 537–40; T. Aldgate, 'British Newsreels and the Spanish Civil War', *History*, 58, Feb. 1973, pp. 160–3.

24. *Documents on German Foreign Policy, 1918–1945*, series D, vol. 1, No. 31, Enclosure; Memorandum of 19 Nov. 1937; CAB 21/740, 24 Nov. 1937.
25. CAB 27/623; F.O. 371/21627 *passim.*
26. F.O. 371/21656, C 1426/42/18; Bialer, op. cit., pp. 201–4.
27. F.O. 371/21628, C 6072/306/602, Foreign Office to Air Ministry, 10 June 1938; CAB 16/201, Sub-committee on limitation of armaments, minutes of 7 July 1938; CAB 21/737, report of Malkin Committee, 15 July 1938; Bialer, op. cit., pp. 204–10.
28. Webster and Frankland, op. cit., vol. 1, pp. 91–2, 95–6, 101.
29. Bialer, op. cit., pp. 210–14.
30. D.P.(P)32(39); Norman Gibbs, *Grand Strategy* (London, 1976), vol. 1, p. 592.
31. D.P.(P)44(39); Gibbs, op. cit., p. 662.
32. S.A.C.13(39).
33. Webster and Frankland, op. cit., vol. 1, pp. 134–5.

5

LIMITED 'CONVENTIONAL' WAR
IN THE NUCLEAR AGE
John C. Garnett

Even a casual reader of this book will already have been made aware, either implicitly or explicitly, that the term 'limited war' is an ambiguous one. Within the literature of strategic studies it is applied to such diverse conflicts as limited strategic wars involving controlled nuclear strikes on the homelands of the Superpowers,[1] and, at the other extreme, it is applied to border disputes and small insurgency wars between minor powers.[2] Deitchman was led to the depressing conclusion that the term referred to almost any military action that did not threaten the *immediate* destruction of the United States and the NATO powers on the one hand, and the Soviet Union and Communist China on the other.[3] Clearly, some conceptual clarification is necessary if the term 'limited war' is to have any analytical usefulness.

One of the most helpful definitions is that of Robert Osgood. 'A limited war is generally conceived to be a war fought for ends far short of the complete subordination of one state's will to another's, and by means involving far less than the total military resources of the belligerents.'[4] By talking about ends and means this definition raises questions about the relationship between the two. Do we fight with limited means because we have limited objectives, or do we settle for limited objectives because we are determined to fight with only limited means?

Now historically, numerous wars have been fought with limited means because the limited objectives of the belligerents simply did not justify the expenditure of unlimited effort to attain them. The typical limited wars of the eighteenth century, for example, were fought in order to achieve marginal adjustments in the balance of power. And, as Osgood has commented, 'the limited value ascribed to the objectives at stake relieved statesmen of the compulsion to wage war to the utmost physical limits'.[5]

But in the nuclear age belligerents may exercise restraint in their conduct of war, not because they have limited objectives, but because they acknowledge that lack of restraint on their part may destroy them both, whatever their objectives. Bernard Brodie had emphasized this point that nuclear states do not fight limited wars because they have limited objectives, but they sometimes settle for limited objectives because on sensible, prudential grounds they are only prepared to expend a limited amount of military effort in attaining them.[6] In other words, it is restraint on *means* rather than ends which is critical to the notion of 'limited war'.

Any satisfactory definition must, therefore, emphasize that limited wars are wars in which opponents exercise deliberate and voluntary restraint in the manner in which they choose to fight. The precise *degree* of restraint that is required for a war to qualify for the adjective 'limited' is uncertain,[7] but what is clear is that if a war is kept small solely because neither side has the capability to wage total war, then it is not really a limited war at all. In the words of Bernard Brodie, 'As a rule we do not apply the term "limited war" to conflicts which are limited naturally by the fact that one or both sides lack the capability to make them total (for example, the colonial war in Algeria).'[8] One of the essential features of limited wars then, is that the possibility of unrestricted conflict must always be present as an obvious and readily available alternative to limited operations.

It follows from this that just because a war is *small* does not mean that it is necessarily limited. Indeed, most of the minor conflicts which have bedevilled international politics since the Second World War do not fit the limited-war category precisely because the belligerents have not practised notable restraint. In these small wars there has been no deliberate hobbling of power that is readily mobilized. As Osgood has pointed out, such wars have been limited, as before the Second World War, only 'by such factors as the limited fighting capacity of the belligerents, the one sided nature of the contest, or the inherent limits of internal war'.[9]

If voluntary restraint on means was a sufficient criterion for establishing the existence of a limited war, then this would suggest that there could be at least two kinds of limited conventional wars; first, limited conventional wars between *conventionally* armed powers, and second, limited conventional wars between *nuclear* powers. Good examples of the former are the 1956 Israeli campaign in the Sinai and the 1962 Indo-Chinese border war. In the Sinai campaign the Israelis launched a pre-emptive strike against Egyptian forces, but their use of military power was both precise and restrained. No attempt was made to conquer Egypt by waging all-out war; no air strikes were made against targets outside Sinai, and no attempt was made to maximize military advantages. In the Sino-Indian war, though both sides made considerable efforts to realize their goals, strict limitations on targetting were observed. No civilians were involved and no attempt was made by either side to cut the other's lines of communication.

Good examples of limited conventional war between nuclear powers or their proxies are the Korean and Vietnam conflicts. In Korea both sides, at least by proxy, had access to nuclear weapons but refrained from using them. In addition, the air battle was confined to the skies over Korea and only industrial targets were attacked. The use of air power against targets close to the Russian and Chinese borders was forbidden, and no attempt was made to impose a naval blockade on mainland China. In Vietnam, similar voluntary restraints were practised, at least by one side. In terms of manpower committed, weapons used, and targets attacked, the United States deliberately refrained from exploiting its readily available military strength.[10]

But most strategic analysts seem agreed that restraint on 'means', though essential to the concept of limited war, is not by itself a sufficient criterion. They have insisted upon adding to it the idea that limited war, properly conceived, must also involve, either directly or indirectly, the policies of the two Superpowers.

As early as 1959 Brodie was moved to suggest that we generally use the term 'limited war' 'to refer to wars in which the United States on the one side and the Soviet Union or Communist China on the other may be involved, perhaps directly but usually through proxies on one or both sides.'[11] Ten years later Osgood reiterated the same thought and hinted that, in the interest of clarity, all those minor conventional or insurgency conflicts in which the Superpowers were not directly or indirectly involved should henceforth be described as *local*, not *limited* wars.[12] More recently, Nordal Åkerman, after reviewing the literature of the subject, was forced to conclude that 'although limited war can be said to exist also at very low levels, the conception would completely lose its special character if the interest of the superpowers were not assumed as an important part of the strategic situation under study.'[13]

Unfortunately, the degree of Superpower involvement that is necessary if a war is to qualify for the term 'limited' is as uncertain as the degree of voluntary restraint that is also required. Both the Korean war and the Vietnam conflict meet the 'Superpower involvement' criterion very clearly, and the various Arab–Israeli wars meet it only slightly less clearly. However, the Indo–Pakistan war of 1947, if not the wars of 1965 and 1971, meets it only minimally, and the various border and civil wars which have formed the bulk of military conflicts since the Second World War do not meet it at all.

Perhaps the main outcome of this semantic exercise is to confirm that although its analytic value is diminished by ambiguity, the most useful and widely accepted definition of 'limited wars' is that they are wars which either directly or indirectly involve one or more of the Superpowers, and in which the belligerents practise restraint by deliberately shackling military power which is mobilized or readily available to them.

Now *conventional* limited wars, which are the main concern of this chapter, are located in the middle of the 'limited war' spectrum of violence; that is to say, they exist below the level of limited nuclear war, be it theatre or strategic, but above the level of insurgency or guerrilla warfare. They are to be distinguished from the former simply by the non-use of nuclear or thermonuclear weapons, and from the latter by the use of *organized* armies engaged in formal battles using *sophisticated* equipment according to *established* tactical and strategic doctrines.

Perhaps it is inevitable that in so far as our concern is with conventional wars which the belligerents have the capacity to make nuclear war should they so desire, our attention is drawn to the nuclear threshold. But the fact that our interest in this 'firebreak' is angled from beneath rather than above means that although we are curious about how and in what circumstances limited conventional wars might be transformed into nuclear wars, we are not much interested in how they are waged once they have become nuclear; that is the subject-matter of Laurence Martin's contribution to this volume.

One of the most important points to remember about limited conventional wars is that they are qualitatively quite different from ordinary conventional wars. Where the belligerents are deliberately refraining from using available military power, the inherent possibility of escalation changes the rules in a profoundly significant way. For example, when an adversary has the power to make a war total and mutually destructive, great care must be taken not to push him too far. In an ordinary conventional battle, if one side achieves a breakthrough, it will probably pursue the retreating forces ruthlessly in order to destroy them or prevent them from regrouping. Having got the enemy on the run, a military commander in an ordinary conventional war would be sorely tempted to follow up his advantage. But in a limited war, this would be a dangerous thing to do, because pursuing an enemy might push him into a corner and make him desperate. A point could be reached when he is so desperate that rather than retreat further he would prefer to escalate the war to a new, higher, and more dangerous level.

In other words, the greater the transformation the winning side seeks, the more plausible is the enemy's threat to escalate. And therefore the winning side, instead of becoming more enthusiastic about its advance, becomes increasingly reluctant to press on for fear of provoking an escalation which will destroy it. Curiously enough, in this situation, the psychological advantage lies with the army which is losing rather than the one which is winning.[14] In fact, in a limited conventional conflict, 'winning' is an inappropriate and dangerous goal; and a state which finds itself close to it should immediately begin to practise restraint.

Another important way in which a limited conventional war differs qualitatively from an unlimited conventional war is in the manner in which troops are deployed on both sides. The troop deployments for waging a conventional war between nuclear opponents are quite different from the normal pattern of troop deployments between belligerents who do not have access to nuclear weapons. It is widely accepted that in a conventional war between nuclear powers, the troops on both sides must be deployed as if they were fighting a nuclear war.[15] The reason for this is that since the belligerents can never be sure that the enemy will not escalate to the nuclear level, they must always be ready for this possibility and must deploy accordingly. In any conventional limited war then, the troops must be deployed as if nuclear weapons are going to be used.

In practice this means that troop concentrations must be avoided in case they are turned into 'killing zones' by an enemy who decides to use tactical nuclear weapons. And yet we know that in conventional combat, in a battle between dispersed forces, the side which is less dispersed gains an advantage. So a military commander in a limited conventional conflict between nuclear opponents faces a real problem. He has the difficult task of avoiding a concentration of his own forces while remaining less dispersed than the enemy. Henry Kissinger once put it this way, 'in a conventional war against a nuclear power, the choice is between accepting military ineffectiveness by employing formations which have been dispersed as if nuclear weapons might be used, or courting disaster by concentrating forces.'[16]

The basic point, which all this is intended to illustrate, is that limited conventional wars are not at all the same as ordinary conventional wars. Limited conventional warfare is a unique form of warfare. The nuclear umbrella which overshadows it makes it qualitatively different from all other sorts of war. The rules of the game have been changed in a very significant way. No matter how violently a limited conventional war is being conducted – and the Korean war was one which was conducted very violently – the combatants will probably be spending at least as much time worrying about the violence held in reserve, as they are with the battle in hand. Henry Kissinger contrasted limited war with all-out war in 1957:

An all out war is relatively simple to plan because its limits are set by military considerations and even by military capacity . . . The characteristic of a limited war, on the other hand, is the existence of ground rules which define the relationship of military to political objectives. Planning becomes much more conjectural, much more subtle, and much more indeterminate, if only because a war against a major enemy can be kept limited only if both parties so desire, and this desire in itself tends to introduce a factor which is outside the control of planning officers.[17]

One of the points which emerges from this is that limited conventional wars must always be considered in the wider context of the unlimited wars into which they may degenerate. The two kinds of war, the one above the nuclear threshold, the other below it, are connected by the knowledge that any conventional war can escalate, either by design or accident, to the nuclear level. It follows from this, that to engage an enemy in limited conventional war, is, by definition, to threaten him, either deliberately or implicitly, with nuclear war. When it is done deliberately, the threat is what Schelling calls 'the threat that leaves something to chance'.[18] In short, when a state engages in limited conventional warfare it is exploiting the risks of total war; it is beginning to rock the boat by setting in motion a process which it does not entirely control and which could therefore lead to nuclear disaster.

It follows from this, that particular tactics in a conventional war must never be judged solely in terms of their conventional military implications. Engaging in the various tactics of conventional warfare is certainly military behaviour, but it may be done for political rather than military reasons, and even when it is done for military reasons it may still have profound political implications.

When, for example, the American government decided to

bomb North Vietnam, part of the aim was to cut supplies to the Vietcong and to damage the war effort of the North. In that sense bombing North Vietnam was a military move with a military purpose. But to think of it solely in those terms would be to seriously misunderstand what was happening, because, fundamentally, the bombing of North Vietnam had a political, not a military purpose. It was intended to hurt the North Vietnamese and to make them comply with American wishes, but it was not intended to defeat them militarily. For that reason, the bombing of North Vietnam has to be evaluated, and indeed only makes sense, in a much wider context than the local military situation in Vietnam.

The Korean war provides us with other examples of military behaviour which only make sense in a much wider political context. Throughout the war the Americans never dropped bombs north of the Yalu river which forms the boundary between North Korea and Manchuria. Now there may have been persuasive military reasons for bombing targets in China – certainly General MacArthur thought there were. But to bomb north of the Yalu would almost certainly have had profound political consequences in terms of Chinese and Soviet involvement in the Korean war. Truman recognized that one bomb north of the Yalu meant something, and its meaning was out of all proportion to its military consequences. Again, to evaluate such an action in purely local, military terms would be absurd, and one might go as far as to say that the parochial perspective of those actively engaged in a limited war is the least relevant of all the perspectives required for fighting it successfully. That basically was why MacArthur had to go. He never really appreciated that, reduced to its essentials, limited war is a political rather than a military activity. He was only one of many soldiers who have found it very difficult to get used to the idea that the object of limited war is not to destroy the armed forces of the enemy, but to communicate with their political masters, to bargain with them by means of a violent, physical dialogue, to engage in what Schelling calls 'coercive diplomacy' and 'tough bargaining'.[19] In an important sense, conventional limited wars are not about winning at all. They are about not losing, and fighting in such a way that the enemy will prefer either a compromise peace or a continuation of the fighting to escalation to the nuclear level.

Because winning is a dangerous goal for both sides, one might expect limited wars either to drag on for many years, or to end in a compromise peace which was satisfactory for neither side but bearable to both. The Korean war ended in a compromise after a relatively short, though very violent, conventional war. By way of contrast, the Vietnam war dragged on for years, and the manner of its termination has perhaps revealed a fundamental weakness in the capacity of Western liberal democracies to wage protracted limited wars. Ho Chi Minh's famous comment, 'You will tire of killing us before we tire of being killed by you', may contain a profound truth about Western societies. It is now widely accepted that the Vietnam war was not lost in Vietnam, but was lost in the United States where an increasingly hostile public opinion eventually forced the American Government to abandon even its limited objectives. The West has not yet learned how to conduct a war which is watched in living-rooms across the country by the wives and mothers of the men who are fighting it.

The Vietnam war revealed that the American people were neither ruthless enough to impose a swift military solution on the lines suggested by Hanson Baldwin,[20] nor resilient enough to fight a lesser struggle over the long haul. These weaknesses may be endemic in Western democracies and they have profound implications for the conduct of protracted limited conventional conflicts. However, in the European theatre at least, there are at least two good reasons for believing that American will and determination may be much stronger. First, because American interests are more easily identified with Western Europe than they are with Vietnam or even Korea. In other words, from an American point of view, a European war is less obviously 'the wrong war, at the wrong place, at the wrong time, with the wrong enemy'. And the second reason why the American government may be firmer in Europe than it was in Vietnam is that the war in Europe is likely to be too short for public opinion about its conduct to be relevant. Putting it bluntly, one way or the other, a European war is likely to be over before the American people have time to tire of it.

Common sense may suggest that the most implausible limited-war scenario of them all is that which envisages a purely conventional war in the European theatre. Yet the search for a limited-war strategy for Europe has quite rightly dominated Western strategic thought since the early 1960s, and the possibility of non-nuclear limited exchanges in Europe has been an abiding preoccupation of limited-war theorists. The rest of this chapter is devoted to an examination of the idea of limited conventional conflict in a European context, and a discussion of its feasibility.

Since the efforts of Secretary of Defense Robert McNamara in the early 1960s, conventional limited-war strategies have been developed as a response to two quite distinct and sometimes contradictory pressures. First, they have been developed because in the event of Superpower deterrence failing, most statesmen have wanted a more sensible alternative to either surrender or annihilation. And second, limited conventional war strategies have been developed because many defence analysts have believed that the ability to wage conventional war actually enhances Superpower deterrence.[21] The main implication of this is that all the theorizing about conventional limited war in the European theatre has to be considered from two quite distinct perspectives – first, from the perspective of those who, in the event of deterrence failing, are interested in waging war in a controlled, non-nuclear way, and second, from the perspective of those deterrent theorists who wish to avoid war altogether.

On the whole those who wish to acquire the capability to wage war in a conventional, non-nuclear way, are fairly pessimistic about the long-term possibilities of avoiding war altogether. Of course they hope that strategic deterrence will work; but they recognize the possibility that it might not. And if deterrence does not work then they believe that it is important to make sure that the war which results does not result in mutual suicide. The argument is that if statesmen acquire the capability to fight below the nuclear level, then there is at least a possibility that they will be able to avoid what Herman Kahn used to call 'spasm war'.

Those who believe that it is possible to avoid war altogether, and who therefore put all of their eggs in the deterrent basket, fall into two categories. There are those who believe that acquiring substantial conventional military capability has the effect of plugging a credibility gap in the deterrent strategy by posing a more credible response to less than massive aggressions. The argument they use is that except in the direst circumstances of an all-out attack on the United States, massive retaliation is an incredible and therefore a poor deterrent, whereas conventional war, because it is a *believable* response is a much more effective deterrent.

The second category of deterrent theorists think very differently. This group regards any improvement in Western conventional capability as very dangerous indeed, because, far from enhancing deterrence, it actually undermines it and makes war more likely. Their argument is that the main reason we have not had an East–West war since 1945 is that the potential aggressors have been terrified by the prospect of global nuclear devastation. Any attempt to make war controllable, or manageable, or survivable by suggesting that it could be waged with conventional weapons, will have the unfortunate effect of bringing war back into the realm of political practicability. Statesmen, no longer terrified by the prospect of Armageddon, will once again regard war as an instrument of policy, and deterrence will have been seriously weakened.

Some of those who have opposed the idea of improving conventional-war capability in Europe on the grounds that it undermines strategic deterrence, have buttressed their position with the argument that the whole idea of limited conventional conflict implies a degree of rationality on the part of decision-makers which is quite unrealistic, and a degree of control of the battlefield which is technically impossible. Human beings are creatures of passion. They have impulses of rage, revenge, frustration, indignation, and pity – all of which make it unlikely that statesmen can conduct war as rationally and coolly as they can play chess. And in situations where power has to be delegated to soldiers operating hundreds of miles away from their political masters, and surrounded by the 'fog of war', it is difficult, if not impossible, for statesmen to exercise sufficient control to keep limited conventional wars limited. Even talking about it is dangerous because it creates an illusion of manageability.

But however dubious the prospects for controlling a conventional war, NATO military doctrine has always acknowledged the possibility of some sort of conventional limited conflict in the European theatre. In 1952 when the alliance adopted the highly ambitious Lisbon goals, it was planning to acquire the capability to fight a prolonged conventional war. Subsequently, and indeed, very quickly, that conventional role was downgraded, and those who have followed the evolution of NATO strategy will be familiar with phrases like 'pause', 'plate glass window', 'trip wire' – all of which reflected a much diminished role for conventional forces in Europe.

The present NATO strategy of 'flexible response' owes much to the efforts made in the early 1960s by Secretary of Defense Robert McNamara, but the most important thing to note about it is that by the time it was adopted by the NATO alliance in 1967 it bore very little resemblance to Mr. McNamara's original conception; in fact, only the words were the same. McNamara was interested in avoiding the stark alternatives of 'suicide or surrender' which were implied by the then current doctrine of 'massive retaliation'. As an alternative he sought to acquire a complete spectrum of military power which would be sufficient to meet any aggression at whatever level it presented itself. In short, McNamara wanted at best to avoid altogether having to take the decision to escalate a European conflict, and at worst, to be able to postpone the decision to escalate for a considerable period of time. In order to implement his strategy he suggested that NATO's conventional forces should be substantially upgraded. In theory at least the strategy had much to recommend it. By raising the nuclear threshold, or lengthening the conventional fuse, it prolonged the non-nuclear phase of the war, and thereby improved the opportunities for reaching a negotiated settlement before the nuclear genie was let out of the bottle. In essence McNamara was pleading for time – for a prolonged period of conventional conflict – which could be used by crisis managers to resolve the political deadlock.

The version of flexible response which was finally adopted by NATO certainly upgraded the importance of conventional forces, but it was an emasculated version of the original. In the event of a major conventional aggression by the Warsaw Pact, there was no thought at all that NATO might avoid escalation to the nuclear level altogether. There was merely an attempt to postpone the decision to escalate – to impose a conventional interval in an East–West war which, if it could not be terminated politically, would have to go nuclear.

And the interval to be imposed before crossing the nuclear threshold was a good deal shorter than that envisaged by McNamara. In 1970 Mr. Healey thought it should be measured in days rather than weeks,[22] and although there is currently some disagreement about the length of time for which NATO is capable of fighting conventionally, most European commentators believe that the conventional phase is likely to be very short.[23] The main point to emerge from this is that it is important to realize that the flexibility implied by the phrase 'flexible response' does not relate to the decision of whether or not to escalate, but only to the timing of the escalation. The relevant question is not *whether* to escalate, but *when* to escalate.

The question of how long a conventional war in Europe will last is an interesting one. In answering it, the first point that has to be made is that it is not entirely a matter of Western choice. If, as is possible, the Soviet Union decides to wage nuclear war from the outset, than NATO will have little choice but to do likewise. In the open literature Soviet military writers naturally start from the assumption that the West would be the first to use nuclear weapons, but the general thrust of their thinking is certainly compatible with the very early introduction of nuclear weapons. As Leon Gouré says, 'Current Soviet theater war concepts . . . pay greatest attention to the nuclear war case in which nuclear weapons would be used to destroy the enemy's theater nuclear capability, his large troop formations, fleets and weapons storage sites, and to "pave the way" for the rapid advance of Soviet troops.'[24] But various observers have detected a quickening of interest in Russian conventional theatre capability,[25] and whilst this should certainly not be regarded as evidence that the Russians now regard conventional war as an alternative to nuclear war in the European theatre, it does imply that they are beginning to believe that conventional operations need not escalate automatically to the nuclear level. John Erickson's balanced interpretation of improving Soviet conventional capability is that it 'must be understood in the context of conducting conventional operations in *the initial phase* of a theater campaign and for *some sustained period*, though, as ever, against that constant nuclear backdrop. In essence, Soviet doctrine and operational practice continues to emphasize the importance of *combined nuclear and conventional operations*.'[26]

There are other aspects of Warsaw Pact planning which suggest that the Russians are thinking in terms of a short conventional phase to any European war. Their tacticians envisage a land battle which would involve swift armoured thrusts by tanks and mechanized infantry penetrating deep into enemy territory. The structure of Warsaw Pact forces suggests that they are designed to peak early in terms of maximum performance. Little effort has been made to give them the logistic support necessary for protracted conventional operations. All the emphasis is on a swift blitzkrieg rather than a prolonged battle.[27] Now if the Warsaw Pact countries do not have the capability to wage a long conventional conflict, it seems sensible to assume that they will avoid it. Their blitzkrieg tactics will either give them an early success or they will go nuclear.

It is interesting to note that by way of contrast NATO conventional forces, at least in terms of their structure and make-up, seem geared for a longer war – between say sixty and ninety days. A high proportion of manpower and resources is tied up in logistic units which, though important in the medium or long term, contribute nothing to the early stages of a conflict. In a conventional, relatively static war lasting for a number of months, NATO might fare quite well, but in a blitzkrieg situation there is a real danger that NATO forces would not be able to survive the initial onslaught by units with a high 'teeth to tail' ratio for long enough to allow the alliance's long-term advantage to take effect.[28] The lesson to be drawn from this is that although it may be important for NATO to acquire the conventional capability to fight for some months without having to escalate, it is even more important that they acquire the capability to survive the first few days. Senator Sam Nunn has been making much the same point in recent months. What is the point of acquiring conventional power capable of surviving for sixty or ninety days, if it cannot survive the first twenty or thirty days? What is the point of building into our force structure an expensive deterrent against a long war if in the process we deny our forces the capacity to endure a short war?[29]

Although the structure of NATO forces in some respects suggests that the alliance may be contemplating a fairly prolonged conventional conflict, there is plenty of other evidence which suggests exactly the opposite. For example, the allies have repeatedly warned the Warsaw Pact countries that because of its inferiority in conventional force levels, NATO would find it necessary to resort to nuclear weapons within a matter of days. Further indications that NATO members believe that the conventional phase will be short are to be found in the Forward Defence Posture which commits the allies to defending Germany as far to the East as is practicable. The German Defence White Paper of 1975/6 hints at the problem where it states 'the initial use of nuclear weapons must be timed as late as possible but as early as necessary' to implement the forward strategy.[30] The problem is that as late as possible and as early as necessary may be very early indeed if Warsaw Pact forces look like making a breakthrough. Understandably, the Germans do not wish to relinquish territory – there is little enough depth in Western Europe anyway – but the price the Germans may have to pay for forward defence may be an early nuclear release.

It is also worth pointing out that many of the current generation of NATO tactical nuclear weapons are very short range. The nuclear artillery has a range of only 20 miles and many of the missiles have a range of less than 100 miles. Obviously, if these weapons are not to be detonated on German territory, they must be used near to the enemy's frontier. Their limited range dictates a forward deployment, and their proximity to the front means that these weapons will either have to be used soon, or pulled back to be used later on German territory, or left to be overrun by the invading Warsaw Pact forces. None of these alternatives has much to recommend it, but it is easy to see that there will be pressure to go nuclear sooner rather than later.

The Forward Defence Posture also generates pressure to initiate nuclear war in the early rather than the later stages of a conventional conflict, because it sees a continuing role for conventional forces even after the nuclear threshold has been crossed. There is a strong feeling in NATO that there is little merit in escalating to the nuclear level only when NATO's conventional forces have been devastated and there is nothing left but a nuclear response. It makes much better sense to initiate a fairly robust or stalwart nuclear defence early on, before NATO's conventional forces have been exhausted. They can then be used later in a counter-attack. For those who are persuaded by this argument, the conventional phase of a European war will be shorter rather than longer.

In truth, nobody knows how long the conventional phase of a European war would last. Indeed, the current NATO doctrine of 'flexible response' makes a virtue of ambiguity on this point. One writer has described 'flexible response' as an 'ambiguous threshold' posture[31] – a posture which involves meeting a conventional attack with a conventional response only up to an unspecified point, after which NATO would cross the nuclear threshold. The fact that the enemy does not know what that point is actually enhances the deterrent threat.

But although no one can be certain how long a conventional war in Europe would last, there is widespread belief – certainly in Europe – that it will be shorter rather than longer. Some deterrent theorists find that a comforting thought. They believe that the lower the nuclear threshold the better the deterrent, and some would like to go even further in this direction than is implied by the present ambiguous strategy. They favour an 'unambiguous threshold posture' which threatens a conventional response to a conventional aggression only up to a publicly specified point after which NATO would initiate the use of tactical nuclear weapons. In other words, those who favour this policy want to take the uncertainty out of flexible response by publicly announcing that a particular level of aggression will automatically trigger a nuclear response. If it adopted this kind of 'unambiguous threshold posture' NATO might, for example, announce to the Soviets that any incursion of over ten miles into German territory would trigger a nuclear war. And in order to make this threat credible it would emplace a line of ADMs exactly ten miles from the frontier. This act, which is an example of what Schelling calls an 'irrevocable commitment' or a 'burning our bridges behind us' kind of act,[32] would make it absolutely clear to the Soviets that any serious incursion into NATO territory would trigger a nuclear response.

Shortening the conventional fuse in this way may appeal to certain deterrent theorists, but most military commentators on the European scene would like to see more, not less, emphasis on NATO's conventional limited war capability. Many of the arguments in favour of improving the alliance's conventional forces revolve around an understandable suspicion that because of the considerable inhibitions against crossing the nuclear threshold, tactical nuclear weapons are unlikely ever to be used. The view is taken that, whatever the NATO guidelines, political leaders, particularly American political leaders, will be very reluctant to cross the conventional/nuclear fire-break, because in their heart of hearts they know it is the only threshold in the escalation process which commands any widespread acceptance. And they also know that once they have crossed the nuclear threshold, they have stepped off a ladder on to a slide which will lead them all too quickly to strategic war.

Politicians are also aware that in the context of Western Europe, a tactical nuclear war is likely to be almost as devastating as a strategic one. In exercise Carte Blanche in the 1950s, 335 nuclear weapons were used with a consequent 1·7 million fatalities and a further 3·5 million casualties. No politician wants to be held responsible for violence on that scale, and it seems fairly safe to assume that they will bend over backwards to avoid it.

And there is at least one more disincentive to going nuclear. The popular assumption that NATO can compensate for a lack of conventional fire power by substituting nuclear fire power may be a very dubious assumption in a situation where the Warsaw Pact also has nuclear weapons available to it. After a tactical nuclear exchange the advantage may very well lie with the side which, because of its manpower advantage, can replace units lost in the field most quickly, i.e. the Warsaw Pact. If this is the case there are good military as well as political reasons for not crossing the nuclear threshold, and for prolonging the conventional phase of a European war.

This kind of reasoning leads inescapably to the conclusion that in the event of a conventional attack by the Warsaw Pact, Europe will probably only be defended conventionally, and this being the case, more conventional military capability is required.

Those who hold this opinion buttress their case with the argument that with a comparatively small amount of effort NATO's inadequacies can be remedied. Although it was once fashionable to talk in terms of overwhelming Warsaw Pact superiority at the conventional level, experts no longer believe that this is the case. Those who have followed recent attempts to estimate the relative strength of NATO's conventional forces when compared to those of the Warsaw Pact may be confused about the details of the analysis. It is now clear that the sums involved in the comparative calculation of military power are both complicated and fraught with uncertainty.[33] But the general drift of the expert argument is clear. NATO is not in anything like such bad shape as we all thought it was. With a little bit of effort, some troop redeployment, some restructuring, some emphasis on militia type forces, some more standardization and so on, NATO's conventional forces could begin to look quite respectable.

And it may be, so the experts tell us, that recent

developments in weapon technology make conventional operations, even against superior odds, a more practical proposition. In very general terms it is suggested that current developments in precision guidance, remote guidance and control, improvements in munitions, in target identification and acquisition techniques – that technological improvements in all these fields will, on the whole, favour defence rather than offence. And that means, of course, that they favour NATO rather than the Warsaw Treaty Organization.[34]

The most significant feature of the new weapons is that they make greater killing power available to small independent units concealed in defensive positions, and that they render more vulnerable any enemy who has to move aggressively across open and unfamiliar terrain. In a situation where these new weapons are available, the opportunities for defensive units to locate and destroy with precision-guided munitions any attacker are much increased. At least one writer has seen possibilities for decentralized and dispersed defensive forces exploiting the advantages of hiding, making it very difficult for an invading army to concentrate for a classic breakthrough. Stephen Canby, with his concept of 'chequer board defence', has outlined tactics whereby small dispersed strongpoints of conventional defence, using man-portable anti-tank missiles might be used to halt armoured thrusts.[35] In general terms, what this amounts to is that there is some evidence that PGMs, improved command and control arrangements, and improved target-acquisition aids, might give numerically weaker NATO forces the ability to counter an infantry, artillery and tank attack by superior Warsaw Pact forces.

Besides improving the single-shot kill probabilities of particular weapons, the new highly accurate conventional munitions hold out the prospect of substantially reducing the collateral damage of an intense conventional war in Europe. This might make it possible to persuade the Germans to move away from the Forward Defence Posture towards a new 'defence in depth' strategy for NATO which might make more military sense.

Now it is very difficult to make firm judgements about some of this new conventional technology and its tactical implications. It is doubtful whether even the experts can have very much confidence in their speculations. The truth is that no one knows very much about conventional limited war in the nuclear age, and many of the weapons we are talking about have never been tested in conditions anything like those which will prevail in a European war. All that we can say, perhaps, is that considered from the rather narrow perspective of war fighting or defence, some of the new technology looks as if it might have favourable implications for the conventional defence of Western Europe.

Considered from the wider but equally important perspective of deterrence, the implications are conceivably less favourable; because, of course, the real danger in improving NATO's conventional 'war fighting' capability is that it may be seen by the Warsaw Pact countries, and also by the European members of NATO, as yet another attempt by the United States to detach its nuclear retaliatory capability from Europe by downgrading the deterrent aspects of the alliance at the expense of improved war fighting capability. The Europeans have always believed that NATO strategy is fundamentally about deterrence, and for that reason they have refused to contemplate limited conventional war except as the first stage of an escalatory process which leads, via tactical nuclear weapons, to strategic nuclear weapons. The European nations have always appreciated that although escalation is a danger that needs to be avoided, it is also a threat which cannot be relinquished, and is, in fact, at the heart of the flexible-response strategy.

In effect the European members of NATO have attempted to deter the Soviets by the following kind of reasoning: 'Don't attack us because even if you do so conventionally, we are so weak that we will have to respond at the tactical nuclear level, and since we don't really control the process of escalation this is quite likely to lead to an American strategic strike which will destroy us all.'

Now the logic of that has never appealed very much to the Americans, who, recognizing their vulnerability to Soviet retaliation, have always been tempted to break the continuous deterrent chain which is implied by flexible response. In order to protect their homelands, the Americans are always tempted to 'decouple' their strategic deterrent from theatre nuclear weapons. They therefore have an interest in persuading the Soviets that the use of tactical nuclear weapons in Europe need not lead to a strategic exchange between the Superpowers. Pressure from the Americans to improve NATO's capability to fight a conventional limited war may be interpreted in Europe as yet another attempt to 'decouple' – this time by breaking the deterrent chain at an even lower level. Improving the conventional capability of NATO may be a way for the Americans to signal to the Russians that a major conventional attack by Warsaw Pact forces will not even provoke a tactical nuclear response, let alone a strategic one. And the tragedy is that even if the Americans do not intend to signal this message, it may still be the interpretation which the Russians put on NATO's attempt to improve her conventional forces. In other words, from the point of view of deterrence, whether it is intended or not, improving NATO's conventional limited war capability may have a dangerous, weakening effect.

This leaves us on the one hand believing that from a strictly military, defensive point of view, a prolonged conventional war may become a more feasible proposition for NATO. And many people would approve of this because it raises the nuclear threshold and improves our chances of keeping a conventional European war conventional. On the other hand, it leaves us with the familiar worry that to the extent that NATO acquires the capability to fight below the nuclear level, this will encourage the Russians to believe that it will not respond above the nuclear level. And that undermines the deterrent posture which is at the heart of NATO strategy.

If there is any single thread running through this discussion of conventional war strategy in Europe, it is that NATO doctrine has never been very clear about the role of the alliance's conventional forces and the sort of conventional limited war they are intended to fight. Perhaps this is because by trying to make conventional forces serve the twin requirements of deterrence on the one hand, and war fighting on the other – concepts which are not entirely compatible – the alliance ends up with a conventional posture which serves neither properly and is therefore ambiguous. Now this ambiguity about NATO's limited conventional war strategy is probably unavoidable in the sense that it is inherent in the strategic dilemmas faced by the West. The really important question is whether we have the *balance* right or whether, in view of changing circumstances, we should now begin to put rather more emphasis on our capacity to fight a limited conventional conflict in the European theatre.

NOTES

1. For a detailed analysis of this variety of limited war see the various essays in K. Knorr and T. Read (eds.) *Limited Strategic War* (London, 1962).
2. Robert McClintock, for example in his book *The Meaning of Limited War* (Cambridge, Mass., 1967) extends his definition of limited war to include both 'wars of national liberation' and 'civil wars'.
3. Seymour J. Deitchman, *Limited War and American Defense Policy* (Cambridge, Mass., 1964), p. 13.
4. Robert E. Osgood, 'The Reappraisal of Limited War' in The Problems of Modern Strategy (Part 1), *Adelphi Paper No. 54* (Institute for Strategic Studies, London, 1969), p. 41.
5. Robert E. Osgood, *Limited War: the Challenge to American Strategy* (Chicago, 1957), p. 63.
6. Bernard Brodie, *Strategy in the Missile Age* (Princeton, 1965), pp. 312–13.
7. Bernard Brodie emphasized the requirement of 'massive restraint' which implied 'no strategic bombing between the United States and the Soviet Union' (ibid., p. 310). However, various other writers have used the term 'limited war' to describe even major nuclear exchanges between the Superpowers. Herman Kahn, for example, would regard a 'controlled general war' between the two Superpowers as a variety of limited war.
8. Brodie, op. cit., p. 309.
9. Osgood, 'The Reappraisal of Limited War', p. 42.
10. For a useful analysis of the deliberate restraints practised in the Korean war, see Morton H. Halperin, *Limited War in the Nuclear Age* (New York, 1963), pp. 39–57.
11. Brodie, op. cit., pp. 309–10.
12. Osgood, 'The Reappraisal of Limited War', p. 41.
13. Nordal Åkerman, *On the Doctrine of Limited War* (Lund, 1972), p. 124.
14. This point is discussed by Henry A. Kissinger in his book *Nuclear Weapons and Foreign Policy* (New York, 1957), p. 168.

15. See, for example, F. O. Miksche, *Atomic Weapons and Armies* (London, 1955) and Otto Heilbrunn, *Conventional Warfare in the Nuclear Age* (London, 1965), pp. 38–88.

16. Kissinger, op. cit., p. 178.

17. Ibid., pp. 140–1.

18. A brilliant analysis of this technique is to be found in T. C. Schelling, *The Strategy of Conflict* (Cambridge, Mass., 1960), pp. 187–203. Reference is also made to it in Schelling's later book *Arms and Influence* (New Haven and London, 1966), pp. 105–9.

19. Schelling's ideas on this subject are most clearly explained in *Arms and Influence*, pp. 1–34.

20. Hanson Baldwin has argued that in Vietnam the Americans made the mistake of not using enough military power in the early stages of the conflict. Their error lay not so much in fighting the war in the first place, but in fighting it at a level which the enemy found tolerable rather than escalating to the point at which the North Vietnamese would have given up. According to Baldwin, any future American intervention must avoid the sin of 'gradualism' by applying overwhelming force at an early stage of the conflict. See Hanson Baldwin, 'The Case for Escalation', *New York Times Magazine*, 22 Feb. 1966, and 'After Vietnam – What Military Strategy in the Far East?', *New York Times Magazine*, 9 June 1967.

21. A useful discussion of this ambiguity at the heart of NATO's Doctrinal Dilemma', *Orbis*, xix (1975).

22. Denis Healey, 'Perspectives of Soviet Military Policy', paper delivered at Sixth International Wehrkunde Encounter Conference, Munich, February 1969, and reprinted under the title 'On European Defence', *Survival*, xi (1969).

23. See, for example, the article by Lord Wigg, *The Times*, 20 Feb. 1969.

24. Leon Gouré *et al.*, *The Role of Nuclear Forces in Current Soviet Strategy* (Miami, 1974), p. 19.

25. See, for example, the essay by W. R. Van Cleave, 'Soviet Doctrine and Strategy', in *The Future of Soviet Military Power*, ed. L. L. Whetton (London, 1976).

26. John Erickson, 'Soviet Theatre Warfare Capability: Doctrines, Deployments, and Capabilities', in Whetton, op. cit., p. 121.

27. Amongst others, R. D. Lawrence and J. Record have suggested that the Soviet military establishment is geared almost exclusively to fighting a short, intense war characterized by offensive operations. See R. D. Lawrence and J. Record, *U.S. Force Structure in NATO* (Washington, 1974).

28. This is the view expressed by Stephen Canby in 'NATO Muscle: More Shadow than Substance', *Foreign Policy* No. 8 (Fall 1972), pp. 38–49.

29. Sam Nunn, 'NATO Strategy', address to the New York Militia Association, 11 Sept. 76, reprinted in *Survival*, xix (1977).

30. *White Paper 1975/1976, The Security of the Federal Republic of Germany and*

the Development of the Federal Armed Forces (Press and Information Office of the Government of the Federal Republic of Germany, 1976).

31. This is the terminology used by D. N. Schwartz in a closely argued article on NATO strategy. See D. N. Schwartz, 'The Role of Deterrence in NATO Defence Strategy: Implications for Doctrine and Posture', *World Politics*, XXVIII (1975), pp. 118–33

32. For a very clear analysis of this technique see Schelling, *Arms and Influence*, pp. 43–9.

33. A good idea of the problems encountered in measuring and comparing military strength is to be gleaned from A. C. Enthoven and K. Wayne Smith, *How Much is Enough?* (New York, 1971). See also R. L. Fischer, 'Defending the Central Front: the Balance of Forces', *Adelphi Paper No. 127* (London, 1976).

34. For a brief discussion of the effects of this new technology on NATO capabilities, see T. Cliffe, 'Military Technology and the European Balance', *Adelphi Paper No. 89* (London, 1972), pp. 19–21. For a more detailed analysis see R. Burt, 'New Weapon Technologies and European Security', *Orbis*, XIX (1975) pp. 514–32, and also J. Digby, 'Precision Guided Weapons', *Adelphi Paper No. 118* (London, 1975).

35. See Stephen Canby, 'The Alliance and Europe: Part IV, Military Doctrine and Technology', *Adelphi Paper No. 109* (London, 1975).

6

LIMITED NUCLEAR WAR
Laurence Martin

The scale of destruction made possible by nuclear weapons is
the chief source of interest in the conception of limited war in
recent decades. There is therefore something of a contradiction
in terms in the notion of limited nuclear war. There were once
voices – that of Edward Teller, for instance – raised to suggest
that there would be self-limiting aspects to nuclear action,
arising from the cost of nuclear weapons and their consequent
reservation for targets of high value, but this belief has been
eroded by subsequent increases in both the number and
variety of nuclear weapons. There are now no longer any
material reasons why nuclear war should not escalate to
catastrophic proportions. Certainly in the popular mind
nuclear weapons are synonymous with destruction on a vast
scale, and for many 'More bang for a buck' still encapsulates
the significance of the nuclear revolution.

This revolution has put the quest for limited war on a new
basis. In previous ages the urge to limit destruction for moral
reasons or to bring sacrifice into some reasonable proportion
to the issues at stake, was reinforced to some degree by the
sheer physical limits on military capabilities. The industriali-
zation of total war in this century had already weakened this
restraint, but nuclear technology has wholly eliminated it.
Henceforth, if the destruction wrought in war is to be curbed,
it will have to be by policies of deliberate restraint. The
potential for disaster is so great that maintaining such restraint
has become the overriding object of great power diplomacy.

For many, the difficulty of defining limits once nuclear
weapons are introduced into conflict has suggested that the
only reliable boundary is that of confinement to non-nuclear
weapons; the so-called nuclear 'fire-break'. This argument has
much force, and although it is interesting and, indeed, highly
necessary, to explore the possibilities of restraint beyond the
fire-break, it must be admitted that, if that juncture were

reached, diplomacy would have proved sadly ineffective and catastrophe would be near.

The first fully nuclear strategy evolved in the West was that of 'Massive Retaliation' under the Eisenhower administration, but the simultaneous development of Soviet nuclear forces raised all the dilemmas of exercising nuclear deterrence under conditions of mutual vulnerability that still plague us. In essence, the fault of this strategy lay in the dual dangers of too much or too little determination, which the critics were to characterize as 'holocaust or humiliation'. Short of abandoning deterrence altogether, the answer could lie only in some idea of limited war.

During the sixties and under the regime of Robert McNamara as United States Secretary of Defense, the emphasis was placed upon the conventional version of limited war. With some misgivings, this policy was endorsed by all the allies but France and was enshrined in the strategy of 'flexible response' formally adopted by NATO in 1967. But the debate aroused by 'Massive Retaliation' during the fifties had also produced two approaches to limited nuclear war.

By far the best known of these was the concept of limiting nuclear action to tactical nuclear weapons, most effectively advocated by Henry Kissinger.[1] This was a new idea in that battlefield nuclear weapons, introduced into Europe progressively from 1952 onwards, had hitherto been thought of merely as an increment to allied fire-power. No new problems of escalation were envisaged because it was assumed that war in Europe would inevitably be total, inevitably involving strategic strikes on the Soviet Union. Introducing the idea of confining nuclear war to the battlefield was an effort to preserve the 'equalising' fire-power of tactical nuclear weapons at a time when growing Soviet retaliatory power made the initiation of strategic nuclear war seem increasingly dangerous and implausible. There was still the hope, however, that uncertainties about the controllability of escalation would preserve a great deal of the overall deterrent effect. Building local defensive capability around tactical nuclear weapons would, it was argued, force the Soviet Union to recognize that a decision for war was a decision to cross the nuclear threshold beyond which, regardless of the new subtleties of doctrine, lay uncharted and dangerous prospects.

Much less widely noted were suggestions that even 'strategic' nuclear war might be limited. These suggestions sought to break the identification of long-range attacks against targets in the Superpowers' homelands with 'countervalue', society-wrecking, city-busting assaults of the kind made familiar by the technologically incompetent bombing offensives of the Second World War and symbolized by Hiroshima and Nagasaki. Attacks should be confined to military targets with the purpose of destroying the enemy's nuclear forces while preserving his cities as a hostage for the immunity of our own. In such a war, a premium would once again be placed on technical advantage and tactical skill, qualities in which the West was thought still to excel even though its nuclear monopoly was lost forever.[2]

To adopt either of these schemes would have required considerable faith in theoretical propositions and the recon-ciliation of many incongruities of interest between the allies. Thus, although elements of both policies were present in the preparations and the rhetoric of NATO during the Kennedy–McNamara era, the main emphasis was on improving the conventional element intended to put the flexibility into the flexible response. Nevertheless, the possibility that the Soviet Union might initiate tactical nuclear warfare prevented NATO from abolishing its own ability to reply in kind and, in any case, while the Western Europeans went along with much of the thought behind the flexible response, they could not contemplate a strategy that offered no alternative to an all-out conventional war that would devastate Europe as surely as one with nuclear weapons. Despite the rhetorical minimization of the nuclear options, tactical nuclear weapons therefore continued to be disseminated in Europe until the renowned number of seven thousand was reached, and debate continued over when they were to be used.

One strand of this debate produced alliance guide-lines on initial and follow-on use of tactical nuclear weapons to achieve a 'military meaningful demonstration of resolve'. The other gradually succeeded in shifting the debate away from demands for more specific American commitments and for greater allied control of the physical means of nuclear action, toward the more relaxed sharing of strategic understanding through the mechanisms of the Nuclear Planning Group established in 1966. Here the effort was to strike a balance between the 'war fighting' role of tactical nuclear weapons and the deterrent effect of their presence as an escalatory link to the strategic nuclear arsenals. More specifically, NATO tactical nuclear weapons were to deter the use of their Soviet equivalents, to be introduced if necessary to bolster a failing conventional defence, and to defeat the Soviet tactical nuclear forces if they entered the battle.

By not insisting on too many clear definitions, a creative ambiguity was preserved. In this way tactical nuclear weapons could simultaneously offer a prospect of escalation sufficiently limited for the United States to contemplate, and sufficiently fraught with escalatory dangers to deter the Soviet Union and thereby reassure the Europeans against the risk of actually having to implement the strategy.[3]

Nevertheless the underlying uncertainties and divergencies of allied interest had not been resolved and the question of what place, if any, limited nuclear action could play in NATO strategy would not go away. Early in the seventies several developments reactivated the debate in a more explicit form than ever before.

The background to these developments was NATO's failure to achieve the highest levels of conventional preparedness called for by the more thoroughgoing advocates of the 'firebreak' and the relative deterioration of the Western position in the face of sustained Soviet military efforts. This failure appeared all the more serious in the light of growing Soviet strategic nuclear power and the explicit acknowledgements of the mutual stand-off at the strategic level embodied in SALT and the declaration of San Clemente. The parallel arms-control negotiations for Mutual Balanced Force Reductions in Europe drew attention to the role of NATO tactical nuclear weapons in offsetting Warsaw Pact advantages in armoured forces and raised the possibility of trading the one for the other. Meanwhile rapid advances in technology, both conventional and nuclear, modified many assumptions about where, even in narrow terms of military effectiveness, the dividing line between conventional and nuclear should be put. Could the new conventional technology raise the nuclear threshold; and if it could, should NATO welcome or deplore the prospect? Finally, the rise of terrorist activity aroused quite new anxieties about the security of tactical nuclear arsenals.[4]

Within the Western alliance the challenge was to preserve the useful ambiguity that reconciled United States fear of escalation to the strategic level with the European anxiety that sustained tactical nuclear action would devastate Europe while affording the Soviet Union immunity and hence freedom from deterrence. Majority opinion seemed to be that this reconciliation would be better preserved the more tactical nuclear weapons could be given a really effective, practical military role to play. If the forces for this role were controllable and discriminating in effect, Europeans might be less afraid to permit their use, Americans might be encouraged by the possibility of a defence that could hold and thus postpone the moment for contemplating strategic action, and the Europeans, in turn, could hope that forces plausibly capable of denying the Warsaw Pact victory on the battlefield would be a substitute for deterrence by threat of strategic retaliation.

Unfortunately the tactical nuclear forces that had been built up during the decade of their doctrinal neglect were rather ill-suited for the kind of limited action called for by this more cautious doctrine. The main defect lay in the high degree of 'collateral' damage that would be caused by anything beyond the most nominal use. Fully to appreciate the damage that Europe might suffer it was necessary to consider the 'aggregate' effects of likely Soviet as well as allied action. But even NATO weapons alone had more than enough destructive potential. Despite the term 'tactical', most so-called weapons were of at least Hiroshima proportions; some had yields of several hundred kilotons. These high yields were not merely the result of some simple-minded love of size; they were the result of other technological weaknesses. The inaccuracy of delivery systems, inadequacies of target acquisition, the long delays and uncertainties in securing permission to fire from the complex command and control mechanisms understandably required for nuclear weapons, all compounded to introduce errors into the process of hitting targets, particularly those that were mobile. Nuclear weapons, however, offered a ready means of rectifying these errors by increasing the yield and therefore the radius of destruction; indeed, in a sense, this was precisely the purpose of nuclear weapons. The consequences for the people and property within the area of this compensatory destruction would, however, be very great indeed. Naturally those who used such weapons had procedures for considering the effect on friendly troops; not until very recently was collateral civilian damage made a part of the tactical calculation.

Technological advances largely conceived in the sixties but brought to the forefront of military attention only in the seventies offer the hope of escape from some of these difficulties. Much the most important is the advent of precision guidance which, while chiefly celebrated as the source for a greater effectiveness in conventional weapons that may make them competitive for some tasks previously thought possible only with nuclear weapons, could also permit large reductions in the yield of nuclear weapons themselves. Further reductions in yields are made possible by 'tailoring' nuclear explosive devices to particular purposes. Much the most publicized of such devices is the enhanced radiation weapon or 'neutron bomb' which, by reducing by a factor of ten the yield necessary to obtain a given dose of prompt radiation, could, over a small range of lower yields, make possible action against enemy troops with much less incidental effect upon unsheltered population around the target and upon surrounding structures. There are, however, other ways of tailoring weapons or adapting delivery systems to maximize intended and minimize unintended effects. Among these are 'minimum residual radiation' warheads, to reduce fall-out from ground-burst weapons, and earth penetrators to achieve underground explosions which, like a pre-emplaced demolition charge, can enhance cratering and once more permit reduction of yields.[5]

None of these technical devices, however, is so important or can be so effective in minimizing collateral damage as a tactical doctrine that seeks to achieve such results. With such a doctrine even familiar weapons could be employed selectively and discriminately; without it not even the most sophisticated weapons will help. Even with the best will in the world many technical problems remain, particularly in the areas of target acquisition and command and control; the latter bedevilled by inherent conflicts between military readiness and political control especially in an environment of potentially great disruption and confusion.

The many unsatisfactory characteristics of existing nuclear strategy led some advocates in the early seventies to propound substantial changes in NATO doctrine.[6] Most of these prescriptions sought to harness the newer weapons becoming available, and the variant most widely debated was undoubtedly the so-called mini-nuke strategy. The term is deceptive, for weapons small in size and yield were by no means novel in conception – although larger ones were more prevalent in the stockpile – and because most developed versions of the proposal called for far more substantial employment of nuclear weapons than the phrase 'mini-nuke' conjured up to the uninformed. What was essential to the new conceptions was the exploitation of plentiful, accurate and controllable nuclear weapons to fight battles.

Many different proposals were lumped under the 'mini-nuke' label. What they had in common was a determination to employ and to categorically threaten the employment of nuclear weapons from the moment battle was joined. These weapons were not to be used in penny-packets to issue dubious signals of determination, but in large numbers to break the enemy offensive. Within variations of individual prescription, the weapons were to be used in the area of the battle and, so far as possible, to limit collateral damage. This, it was argued, would have both deterrent and defensive advantages. The certainty of nuclear response, made more so perhaps by the run-down of NATO's conventional defences, would increase deterrence not so much by arousing fears of escalation – those who suggested limited damage could not comfortably play that card – but by the threat of an impenetrable defence. The use of weapons early, while friendly forces were intact, command and control unimpaired and many enemy targets still in known locations, would maximize military effect.

Some American advocates of prompt tactical nuclear response had as an objective the 'decoupling' of United States strategic forces from the defence of Europe. Only thus, they thought, could the United States still credibly threaten such action. To expose the United States itself to nuclear attack, they believed, was more than the American interest in European security could justify. Other Americans believed that the advent of strategic nuclear parity and the contemporary progress of SALT had, for good or ill, already effectively decoupled strategic forces. To make this clearer, some versions of tactical nuclear strategies suggested that all but the shortest-range, battlefield systems should be withdrawn from Europe, so that the Soviet Union could not mistake the engagement of the tactical weapons for the onset of strategic attack. This proposal, of course, coincided very closely with the drive against the 'forward based systems' launched by the Soviet Union in SALT.

The various proposals for more precipitate, indeed virtually automatic, use of tactical nuclear weapons naturally horrified those who found intolerable any suggestion that nuclear wars might actually be fought or who feared that the idea that the consequences of nuclear combat could be limited would erode the vague aura of catastrophe that makes the mere existence of nuclear weapons a source of caution. There were, however, more specific sources of scepticism. Among these was doubt as to whether nuclear weapons, even of the most modern kind, would in fact constitute an effective defence within the damage limits specified. Some estimates suggested that very large numbers of weapons would be required; as many as a thousand 2-kiloton weapons being cited to deal with six tank divisions. The vaunted enhanced-radiation weapons only reduced collateral damage over a very limited range of yields, roughly the effective equivalent of 10–30 kt of normal weapons. No amount of warhead design could eliminate the gross errors entailed in poor target identification or bad command and control. Nor could a battlefield strategy escape the disadvantage that the battle was almost certain to be on

friendly territory. One of the more vigorous French advocates
of tactical nuclear weapons faced this problem squarely:
'Better to accept a Verdun-like landscape on the ten to twenty-
mile depth of friendly territory which would be the nuclear
dam, than battle in depth an invasion.' But this was not an
encouraging prospect for any West German.[7]

The damage that NATO might do to itself, however,
becomes insignificant when compared to the damage an
uninhibited Soviet counterstroke might do. Thus expectations
about Soviet tactical nuclear policy are a fundamental element
in the evaluation of Western proposals. Unfortunately, while
evidence about Soviet intentions is ambiguous, the general
tenor is not encouraging for those who would like to justify the
practicability of limited nuclear war.

For most of the nuclear era the dominant Soviet view has
apparently been that war with the West would inevitably
involve nuclear weapons and would see the joint employment
of all means, conventional and nuclear, both tactical and
strategic. During periods when the Soviet Union lacked the
American variety of nuclear weapons, this scorn for the
smaller weapons may have contained an element of bluff. But
once the Red Army acquired its own tactical weapons there
was still no sign that it was interested in keeping nuclear war
limited to lower yields or to the immediate battlefield. On the
contrary, the early and extensive use of nuclear weapons was
held to be the best way of breaking through a defence: either
the defensive enemy concentrations would be annihilated or
the defender, dispersing to avoid such a fate, would offer easy
lines of penetration. Moreover, the problems of maintaining
command, control, and troop safety in a prolonged nuclear
engagement also led the Russians to prefer a sharp, thorough,
and early bombardment of both forward defences and rear
installations, particularly nuclear. After this, Soviet forces
could grapple with the defenders so closely as to inhibit
retaliation. It is this doctrine of prompt expenditure of perhaps
half the Soviet arsenal of theatre nuclear weapons that led to
Soviet doctrine being characterized in the West as 'deep and
dirty'. To quote but one Soviet pronouncement: 'in the
military, one cannot be guided by the principle of "better late

than never". Prediction in military affairs, particularly when one takes into consideration a potential nuclear missile war, should correspond in full to the principle of "the sooner the better".[8]

In earlier years of Soviet debate it was generally assumed that this extensive theatre nuclear war would proceed simultaneously with a strategic war. But in the seventies, with the advent of nuclear parity and a clear United States reluctance to contemplate all-out nuclear war, some new notes entered Soviet discussions. As revealed by Soviet eagerness to limit the so-called forward based systems in SALT – that is, those weapons based in the European theatre that could hit the Soviet Union – while excluding their own medium-range missiles and aircraft capable of operating all over Western Europe, the Soviet Union saw the possibility of decoupling a theatre-wide nuclear campaign in Europe from mutual attacks on the homelands of the Superpowers. This is, of course, the worst European nightmare so vehemently depicted by General de Gaulle. For while the original Soviet conception of war in Europe faced up with fortitude to the prospect of widespread nuclear action, that realism must also have exercised a sobering influence on Soviet calculations about the risks of launching an attack. The decoupled version would offer the Soviet Union a nuclear war of limited liability. Decoupling would also help the Soviet Union to deal with the nuclear element in NATO's own declared defensive strategy. If the NATO doctrine of resorting to theatre nuclear weapons if conventional defence fails retains any credibility, the Soviet Union cannot be sure that even confining its own operations to conventional weapons would avert the outbreak of nuclear war. Soviet policy must therefore concentrate upon trying to minimize the effects of such a war upon the territory of the Soviet Union.

It is true that in the seventies Soviet military writers have discussed the possibility that, for political reasons, at least the early stages of war in Europe might be wholly conventional. These writings, together with exercises without nuclear weapons and the steady build-up of Warsaw Pact conventional capabilities have led some Western analysts to conclude that conventional war has become the dominant Soviet conception.

This seems too confident a conclusion. Clearly the Red Army is studying the problems of conventional war employing the most modern weapons. But as the Soviet conception of nuclear war also calls for intense conventional operations to accompany and follow up the nuclear strikes, too much should not be read into either the doctrinal discussions or the provision of the appropriate weapons for conventional action. Moreover Soviet theatre nuclear weapons have also received careful attention and some developments, such as imitation of Western self-propelled nuclear-capable artillery, suggest a continued expectation that war would be nuclear. The most one can say with confidence in the late seventies is that the Soviet Union is giving much more serious attention than ever before to the possibility that nuclear war might be subjected to some restrictions, and that within these the Soviet Union might be able to win a victory without unacceptable damage to itself.[9]

Putting Soviet and NATO doctrine together leads on balance to the conclusion that if war comes in Europe it is very likely to be nuclear. To believe otherwise requires great confidence in Soviet willingness to gamble on conventional victory and in NATO's lack of determination to implement its strategy of nuclear escalation. This diagnosis must, if shared by the Soviet Union, exercise a considerable deterrent effect upon any aggressive tendencies. It is quite clear, however, that no amount of esoteric strategic argument will persuade the NATO governments to draw the conclusion that all they need is a nuclear tripwire. Conventional forces are thought to offer several indispensable options. Among these are the ability to deal with the early, possibly unintended, stages of conflict without facing the nuclear decision, and to create thereby an armed mêlée within which the possibility of hotblooded or semi-accidental recourse to nuclear weapons might seem more plausible. Above all, allied governments of various political persuasions have made it quite clear that they are unwilling to make the surrender of political discretion to use or withhold nuclear weapons that the strategy of prompt use would entail. Even such a person as M. Chirac, speaking from the Gaullist tradition, has said that 'we must provide ourselves with the wherewithal for a defence which is more subtly graduated' and that we must 'not renounce all versatility'.[10]

Such a view does not mean the rejection of the use of nuclear weapons. On the contrary, it entails developing as many options for limited nuclear action as possible to make the threat of action plausible. Unlike the more extreme advocates of reliance on nuclear weapons, however, NATO governments insist on extending this flexibility into the conventional area. This is true, at least, so far as doctrine goes. Whether NATO actually provides itself with the appropriate range of physical capabilities is another question.

Given Soviet willingness to contemplate nuclear war and their recent interest in limiting it to the European battlefield – even though broadly defined – it becomes a vital NATO and particularly Western European interest to inhibit as many Soviet options as possible. Clearly the most important objective is to thwart the Soviet effort to decouple the strategic forces from the theatre war. Here the European national nuclear forces have a role to play but the most effective deterrent remains the United States strategic force. Keeping these forces coupled, however vaguely, to the European theatre is the pre-eminent reason for accepting American insistence on the preservation of a flexible, including conventional, response.

The task of deterring the use of nuclear weapons – until NATO itself wants to introduce them – is perhaps simpler than that of maintaining limits on their employment after the nuclear phase begins. Sheer degradation of control mechanisms on both sides during combat poses problems that have not yet been overcome and on which technological ingenuity might be more profitably spent than on weapons. It is also essential for NATO to retain the capacity to match any Soviet extension of nuclear action beyond the immediate battlefield. Soviet incentives to strike deep into Western Europe may be the greater the more NATO's own nuclear weapons are vulnerable to pre-emptive attack. Thus improvements in the 'survivability' of NATO's nuclear weapons may help limit Soviet action both by reducing incentives for deep attacks and by preserving the capacity for theatre-wide retaliation. The decision in the early seventies to assign submarine-based nuclear weapons to theatre operations serves both these purposes but also introduces further complex questions about the relationship between the theatre and strategic systems.

From this perspective the role of technological improvements and doctrinal refinements related to tactical or theatre nuclear war is not to create a new, wholly distinct level of limited nuclear war, but to make this intermediate level of conflict a more practical way of defending allied territory without divorcing it from the higher levels of deterrence or the lower levels of conventional response. This is the threefold formula of defence and deterrence; conventional, theatre-nuclear and strategic-nuclear, sometimes referred to as 'the NATO Triad'.

The concept of the 'Triad' illustrates very well the paradoxical nature of the search for a doctrine of limited nuclear war. For the tactical or theatre-nuclear element, which is by definition a limited concept, depends for its limitations upon a link to the limitless possibilities of the strategic balance. It is consequently not surprising that in the seventies, given the emphasis on strategic parity and mutual vulnerability in SALT, interest has revived in attempting to discover limited ways of conducting strategic nuclear war.

By far the most noted expression of this search was the idea of 'limited strategic options' enunciated in 1974 by James Schlesinger, the United States Secretary of Defense.[11] Some aspects of this doctrine had been foreshadowed by the concepts of 'city-sparing' developed in the fifties and by the 'counter-force' period of McNamara's policy embodied in his famous speech at Ann Arbor in 1962, when he called for a strategy in which 'principal military objectives, in the event of a nuclear war stemming from a major attack on the Alliance, should be the destruction of the enemy's military forces, not of his civilian population.'[12] But whereas these earlier notions – later abandoned in favour of the allegedly stabilizing principle of 'mutual assured destruction' – had envisaged a full-scale military struggle waged without total destruction of civilian society, the latter-day idea of limited strategic options calls for much more restricted nuclear strikes as a way to exercise nuclear power for less than total stakes. In Schlesinger's words: 'What we need is a series of measured responses to aggression which have some relation to the provocation, have prospects of terminating hostilities before general nuclear war breaks out, and leave some possibility for restoring deterrence.'[13] The same idea had been simmering during the earlier years of the Nixon–Kissinger foreign policy, best expressed in President Nixon's 1971 *Foreign Policy Report*: 'I must not be – and my successors must not be – limited to the indiscriminate mass destruction of enemy civilians as the sole possible responses to challenges. This is especially so when that response involves the likelihood of triggering nuclear attacks on our own population.'[14]

This line of thought clearly indicated a search for ways to make strategic nuclear action compatible with purposes other than the merely vengeful and complete destruction of the Soviet Union in retaliation for an equally unrestrained attack on the United States. The threat of such an unlimited retaliation is probably an essential ultimate deterrent against such a Soviet attack, but it cannot plausibly be related to lesser provocations. It may, however, be possible to design more limited strategic attacks that can be credibly linked to smaller stakes and less vital interests. One such stake, less important to the United States than its own survival but nevertheless of immense significance, is the continued independence and survival of Western Europe, and one occasion for limited strategic retaliation might well be the escalation of theatre nuclear warfare beyond limits tolerable to the Western Europeans. The search for limited strategic options is therefore in one respect a quest for a strategy the United States can plausibly threaten to implement on behalf of its friends; an effort to keep 'extended deterrence' alive under conditions of nuclear parity. Indeed Dr. Schlesinger made this explicit by delaring that the United States strategic force 'is certainly still coupled to the security of Western Europe; that is a major reason behind the change in our targeting doctrine.'[15]

Desire to retain the nuclear initiative has not, however, been the only motive behind the search for limited strategic nuclear options. The increase in quantity and quality, and especially accuracy, of Soviet strategic nuclear forces has also aroused American fears that the Soviet Union might undertake limited strategic strikes of its own. Broad equality with the United States might make the Soviet Union optimistic that an all-out United States retaliatory attack was unlikely while the increasing variety, payload, and accuracy of Soviet intercontinental systems might give the Soviet Union the ability to make limited attacks of precisely the type envisaged in the 'Schlesinger doctrine'. Even more disturbing is the fear that the Soviet Union might in a crisis undertake a full-scale 'disarming' attack on the United States land-based strategic forces, now deprived by the first SALT treaty of any active defences. Given the persistent refusal of Soviet theorists to be moved by American notions of deterrence by 'assured destruction' and their preference for regarding even strategic nuclear conflict in terms of offence and defence with the possibility of 'winning', it could be argued that limited strategic war fits Soviet philosophy better than American. Soviet enthusiasm for such traditional activities as civil defence points in the same direction.

Not surprisingly, overt Soviet reaction to Dr. Schlesinger's proposals has been extremely hostile. In a typical article entitled 'The Problem of the Inadmissability of a Nuclear Conflict' two Soviet authors insisted that 'In a word, unbiased analysis indicated that the quest for ways of making "limited" use of nuclear weapons both strategically and tactically is fraught with dangerous consequences.'[16] But while this is an understandable reaction to a strategic departure that would solve some NATO problems and thwart the Soviet effort to decouple American strategic forces from European security, it by no means follows that the Soviet Union would refuse the opportunity to limit the consequences if war did begin.

Upon these assumptions the United States needs the nuclear options advocated by Dr. Schlesinger for both positive and negative reasons. According to their advocates, such options require chiefly some alteration of doctrine and of declaratory policy rather than new equipment, though improved command and control mechanisms and an adequate supply of accurate weapons would be necessary to afford flexibility and permit the discretionary action that alone could hope to induce corresponding restraint on the Soviet side.

The targets involved in such limited strategic strikes could range from a widespread attack on strategic nuclear systems to limited attacks on other military installations or on key industrial plants. Quite clearly warfare of this kind would be extraordinarily provocative and perilously close to the moment of uncontrolled escalation. Strategic analysts have scarcely begun to ponder the immense implications of weakening the assumption that strategic nuclear action would necessarily be synonymous with holocaust. Moreover, as with suggestions that new standards of accuracy may make strategic bombardment with conventional warheads practicable, the concept of limited strategic nuclear war opens up the little-discussed relationship between the thresholds of nuclear action and of attacks upon the territory of nuclear powers. Where on the ladder of provocativeness or deterrent effectiveness are the steps of using nuclear weapons, breaking the sanctuary of nuclear powers' territory, and doing the latter with nuclear weapons albeit in limited fashion? Moreover, very practical strategic questions are raised once the notion of less-than-total nuclear war is accepted, for such measures as civil defence, dispersal of industry, and active anti-aircraft and anti-missile defences could regain much of their attraction. Many familiar problems of strategic thought once thought to be permanently irrelevant to the nuclear age would again require anxious consideration.

The combination of new technology and evolving doctrine for both strategic and theatre nuclear operations has made the late seventies an unusually active phase in the evolution of the idea of limited nuclear war. What the outcome of this activity will be is far from clear. Because the discussion of such novel strategic possibilities so readily becomes abstract and divorced from real political circumstances, it is perhaps necessary to reiterate that no one can sanely doubt that any conflict between great powers which proceeds to the stage of nuclear warfare will be near to a catastrophic outcome. Of necessity none of the proposals for controlling such a conflict are based on experience and their merits are wholly speculative.

It is impossible to refute entirely the criticism that the various strategies of limitation may appear to make the world safe for nuclear warfare and thereby hasten its onset. There is also force in the argument that, whether or not there is an actual nuclear war, the development of strategies for the limited use of nuclear weapons and the consequent demonstration that they are thought to be useful political instruments, may accelerate the process of nuclear proliferation. How serious these dangers are cannot be determined, not merely because we cannot know how far the fears will be realized, but also because we cannot evaluate the dangers facing the world if nuclear weapons continue to be thought of as merely sterilized instruments of mutual strategic deterrence between a few nuclear powers.

So long as nuclear weapons exist at all, the danger of nuclear war will also persist. It would be absurd to believe that such powerful means of destruction can be wholly and permanently divorced from political conflicts. The question thus becomes in what way can this linkage best be handled so as to minimize conflict and, above all, to avert all-out nuclear war. Limited nuclear war thus presents a familiar dilemma: how to steer a course between relatively manageable strategies for employment and the horrifying prospects of catastrophe, so as best to preserve the deterrent and stabilizing influence of the nuclear balance?

To regard nuclear war entirely as something too horrible to contemplate and to evolve no strategies more subtle than all-out mutual annihilation would lead towards paralysis in crisis and vulnerability to nuclear blackmail by more stout-hearted or reckless opponents. At most it might lead to a precipitate descent into catastrophe for lack of a better alternative to surrender.

There is therefore a powerful case for contemplating how, if a nuclear war came, it could best be waged so as to salvage as much as possible on both sides from the disaster; to carry into the war that spirit of grudging mutual self-interest that has produced the achievements of the last two decades of arms control. These have been limited but, under the novel incentives of the nuclear age, they have been considerably more ingenious and impressive than those of earlier periods. The proper question may therefore be not, should we contemplate limited nuclear war, but, should we consider ways of limiting the nuclear war which is henceforth always a possibility?

NOTES

1. Chiefly in his *Nuclear Weapons and Foreign Policy* (New York, 1957).
2. Perhaps the earliest and soon forgotten exposition of this was Richard Leghorn, 'No Need to Bomb Cities to Win Wars', *U.S. News and World Report*, 28 Jan. 1955.
   See also Klaus Knorr and Thornton Read (eds.), *Limited Strategic War* (New York, 1962).
3. For fuller discussion of these points see Laurence Martin, 'Theatre Nuclear Weapons and Europe', *Survival*, Nov./Dec. 1974 and 'Flexibility in Technical Nuclear Response' in Johann Holst and Uwe Nerlich, *Beyond Nuclear Deterrence* (New York, 1977).
4. The most influential demand that these problems should be faced was 'Policy, Troops and the NATO Alliance', Report of Senator Sam Nunn to the Committee on Armed Services, 2 April, 1974. James Schlesinger's ultimate answer was in *The Theater Nuclear Force Posture in Europe, A Report to the Congress*, 1 Apr. 1975.
5. See the section 'Promises of Technology' in Holst and Nerlich, op. cit.
6. From a vast body of literature see W. D. Bennett, R. R. Sandoval, and R. G. Shreffler, 'A Credible Nuclear-Emphasis for NATO', *Orbis*, Summer 1973; Colin S. Gray, 'Deterrence and Defence in Europe: Revising NATO's Theatre Nuclear Posture', *Strategic Review*, Sept. 1975, and D. G. Brennan, 'Alternative Tactical Nuclear Force Postures' (Hudson Institute, N.Y., 1975).
7. Colonel Marc Geneste in an interview with Dr. David Yost (Ph.D. dissertation, University of Southern California, 1976).
8. A. S. Milovidov, *The Philosophical Heritage of V. I. Lenin and Problems of Contemporary War* (Moscow, 1972) U.S. Air force translation, Washington, D.C., 1975, p. 261.
9. For the Soviet debate see Joseph D. Douglass, Jr., *The Soviet Theater Nuclear Offensive*, published for the U.S. Air Force (U.S. Govt. Printing Office, Washington, D.C., 1976); A. A. Sidorenko, *The Offensive* (Moscow, 1970), U.S. Air Force translation, Washington, D.C., 1974.
10. M. Chirac, *Défense Nationale*, May 1975, reprinted in *Survival*, Sept./Oct. 1975.

11. See his press conference, 10 June 1974, *Survival*, Mar./Apr. 1974; *Report of the Secretary of Defense*, 14 Mar. 1974, pp. 25ff.; Laurence Martin, 'Changes in American Strategic Doctrine: An Initial Interpretation', *Survival*, July/Aug. 1974.
12. 16 June 1962; partial text, *Survival*, Sept./Oct. 1962.
13. *Report of the Secretary of Defense*, 14 Mar. 1974, p. 38.
14. *U.S. Foreign Policy for the 1970's*, 25 Feb. 1971, p. 70.
15. In B.B.C. discussion with Laurence Martin, Radio 4, 24 Oct. 1974.
16. M. A. Milshteyn and L. S. Semeyko, 'The Problem of the Inadmissibility of a Nuclear Conflict (On New Approaches in the United States'), *USA* (Moscow), reprinted in *Strategic Review*, Spring 1975.

7

LIMITED WAR AT SEA SINCE 1945
D. P. O'Connell

All conflicts that have occurred since the Second World War may be classified as 'limited wars', but it is important to ascertain what exactly that expression imports. Some of these conflicts have been limited in the areas in which they have occurred, although, as in the cases of Korea, the Middle East, and the Indo-Pakistan wars, not in the scale of operations or the level of weaponry; while others have been limited in all of these aspects. Some have been incidents while others, like Vietnam, have been protracted episodes. Even incidents have been unlimited in respect of firepower – as when the Chinese navy sank a South Vietnamese warship in 1974 in a dispute over occupation of the Paracel Islands – although they have been limited in duration, while episodes have been character-ized by a low level of weaponry.

There have been roughly one hundred situations since 1945 in which naval power has been exerted in a coercive role, involving about fifty different navies. Each of these could be described as 'limited', although they have varied enormously in the scale of intensity or the level of violence. The factor common to them all is the limited operational goal, not the way the parties have conducted themselves. Strategic options in the contemporary world are more restricted than formerly because the political circumstances have changed. War is no longer an option, and hence the political goal of subjugation is no longer available to those who seek to influence others. That limitation upon strategy requires limitations upon tactics too, so that there are curbs upon the deployment and use of the vehicles of warfare that were unfamiliar to previous ages.

If war is no longer a political option, how are the conflicts which have occurred, and continue almost daily to occur, to be rationalized? The answer is that they are justified on the theory of 'self-defence' by both sides, and it is this that enables us to assimilate the one hundred-odd naval incidents since

1945, so diverse in character and degree of violence, for the purpose of analysis. 'Self-defence' is a concept of international law, and one endowed with certain qualifications and conditions by the law which politicians have to take into account. The rules of 'self-defence' provide us with a framework within which all of the operations that have occurred since 1945 can be brought, so that a discussion of them can rise above mere anecdote, and some useful political strategic and tactical principles may be formulated on the basis of a study of them.

A review of the rules of 'self-defence' thus appears to be the fundamental purpose of a study of 'limited war', since these provide the common thread running through the uses of force in the contemporary world. No government is in the political position to act coercively without having to justify its conduct in the United Nations; and few governments are in the position to do so without taking into account the system of its own political and regional alliances, and the forum of its own public opinion. To gain its ends by resort to force, then, any government must be in a position to present a plausible case that it is the subject of illegal coercion. To be in that position, it must accept limitations as to its conduct, the locations of its conduct, and the scale of its conduct.

This is not just a matter of rephrasing the doctrine of the 'just war'. While it may be true that every nation that has resorted to war in modern times may have pleaded the justice of its cause, the justice of the cause imposed no serious restrictions as to goals or means: the just war authorized war; 'self-defence' authorizes nothing more than 'self-defence'.

This fundamental shift in international relations is reflected in two paragraphs of the United Nations Charter that stand in uneasy conjunction. Article 2 (4) outlaws the use of force, and does so in plain, absolute, and peremptory terms. If it stood alone there would be no plausible justification within the framework of United Nations membership for resort to force. But it stands in relation to Article 51, which reserves the inherent right of individual or collective self-defence if an armed attack 'occurs'.

Each of the words in Article 51 has been the subject of

controversial exegesis, which it is at present unnecessary to recall. The central point of the Article is that it warrants the resort to force in some circumstances, but always against an 'armed attack'. What is an 'armed attack'? Is it literally the unleashing of forces or weapons, so that preventive resort to force is not 'self-defence'? If that is the case, is pre-emption a tactical option forbidden to the military?

These questions have become central to naval planning, and will require further discussion. But alongside them are other questions raised by Article 51. If the right of self-defence is, as the Article says, 'inherent', does it import the classical doctrine of pre-1945 international law that self-defence, to be justified, must be limited to what is 'necessary and proportional' in order to defend oneself? These concepts, necessity and proportion, embody limitations upon conduct, and these can be classified for the purpose of analysis into limitations as to:

(a)   the theatre of operations;
(b)   the scale of operations and the level of weaponry;
(c)   The graduation of force and the scale of response.

All of the one hundred-odd naval operations since 1945 have been characterized by the factor of such limitation. To begin with the theatre of operations: until 1945 all wars at sea were fought without inherent geographical limitation. Indeed, the contrary was the case: seapower was best deployed to destroy an enemy's sea-borne commerce and deny him access to the sea as an avenue of communications and strategic advantage. Although the opportunities for the flexible use of seapower in waters distant from the focus of conflict have been available, they have not, since 1945, in fact been taken advantage of.

For example, Portugal might have seized Indian shipping anywhere around the globe at the time of Goa. The United States might have seized North Korean shipping anywhere at the time of the Pueblo incident. Arab countries, because of uncertainty as to their negotiating stance, were tentative about efforts to blockade Israeli shipping outside the immediate area of conflict. In fact, none of the limited wars at sea since 1945 has spilled over into the oceans at large.

The formal reason for this is that such an extension of the

conflict could not plausibly be presented as necessary and proportional to resist an armed attack, but behind that reason lies the incubus of world opinion, which, rightly or wrongly, has been supposed by naval planners and their political masters to be tolerant towards localized conflict but apt to be dangerously alarmed by eruptions of violence in the sea-lanes of international commerce. The advantages of seapower in this respect are thought to be outweighed by the disadvantages of political complications and embarrassment.

Whether the localization of the conflict at sea is a legal concept or merely a matter of prudence is a moot question. In the context of the Middle East conflicts it has been treated as a legal rule. When the Israeli destroyer *Eilat* was sunk by Styx missiles fired from alongside in Alexandria, it seems to have been a common and unquestioned assumption in the ensuing Security Council debate that the limit of the territorial sea is the legal limit to the use of force in self-defence. Israel sought the denunciation of Egypt on the contention that the *Eilat* was in the high seas when attacked, whereas Egypt defended her action on the contention that she was in Egyptian territorial waters, and so constituted a military invasion of Egyptian territory.

The circumstances of this incident are perhaps better classified as 'law-enforcement' than as limited war. The action occurred four months after the Six Days' War, and was thus isolated from any phase of open conflict. In the circumstances it would certainly have been illegal for Egypt to attack an Israeli warship in the high seas, but not necessarily illegal for it to resist an incursion into its own territorial waters of a warship not engaged in innocent passage. Whether the same restraint would operate in the case of limited war is not so clear: In fact, in the Six Days' War naval engagements occurred outside of territorial waters, although in the location of the main conflict.

Whether or not the restriction of naval operations to the territories, or at least the waters adjacent to the territories of the combatants, is a matter of law or merely a matter of political self-denying ordinance, it is a characteristic of the limited goals of contemporary conflict. How strictly the restraint is observed will obviously depend upon the geographical location and the political circumstances. In Vietnam the United States was under great political constraint, both internationally and at home, as to the nature of the conflict, and hence as to its location. It was politically necessary to put the whole matter on the basis of law-enforcement, and to avoid the appearance of retaliation or reprisal. In the Indo-Pakistan conflict of 1971 there were far fewer inhibitions because world sympathy had been engaged in favour of the independence of Bangladesh. The differing circumstances are reflected in the different naval policies adopted in the two cases.

In Vietnam two separate naval operations were set up. One, Operation 'Market Time', was limited to the distance of twelve miles off the coast of South Vietnam, that is, south of the DMZ. The other, Operation 'Sea Dragon', was limited to the distance of twelve miles off the coast of North Vietnam. Although the distances were the same, the operational concepts, due to different political and legal considerations, were quite different. Operation 'Market Time' was concerned with policing the three-mile territorial sea limit of South Vietnam and an additional nine-mile contiguous zone. The Seventh Fleet derived its legal competence in this law-enforcement operation from legislation of South Vietnam. This paraphrased the relevant provisions of the Geneva Convention on the Territorial Sea and Contiguous Zone, which subjects the territorial sea to sovereignty and the contiguous zone to the power to prevent infringements of the law relating to customs and immigration. The latter was construed to cover infiltration of arms, supplies, and personnel.

Operation 'Sea Dragon' was an action based on the concept of self-defence. It accepted the claim of North Vietnam to a twelve-mile territorial sea, and treating that as an area of sovereign waters, relied upon the same principle in the case of naval operations as in the case of the bombing of North Vietnam, namely, that this was necessary and proportionate harassment and interdiction of the logistic support for Communist 'armed attack' on South Vietnam.

The difference in the two concepts implied differences in

operational conduct. In the area of Operation 'Market Time' rules of engagement and operational orders had to take into account the right of innocent passage through the territorial sea, the extent of the power of visit and search in the contiguous zone, and the right of hot pursuit from each of these areas. The rules of international law are difficult and complex in these matters, and these difficulties and complexities were perforce inducted into operational orders. In the case of Operation 'Sea Dragon', the right of innocent passage had to be observed, but since practically speaking the only foreign shipping to be found in North Vietnamese territorial waters would be in transit to or from Haiphong and other northern ports which were excluded from the area of operations, this proved not to be a difficult problem. All shipping in lateral transit along the coast, generally speaking, could be assumed to be North Vietnamese, but it was not to be attacked unless the indices of logistic support for the war were verified. That left fishing-boats immune from attack.

Apart from the locations in which force might be used, and the degree of force, there were restraints common to both Operations from their very nature. Merchant shipping as such could not be taken in prize. Attack on civilians had to be avoided in order to comply with the laws of war and the Red Cross Conventions, but this rule had to be more strictly observed than in ordinary warfare. The distinctions between military and civilian targets, and between attack and harassment and interdiction, put a premium upon positive identification which was unusually strict.

The legal justifications for these two Operations provided no right of belligerent operations more than twelve miles at sea, other than the right of self-defence against naval or air attack. The operational orders concerning this had to face up to the question, not only of positive identification, but of pre-emption. In fact, on the very few occasions when North Vietnamese aircraft strayed outside of the twelve-mile limit they were taken under fire, which shows that it may be impossible in a conflict of that scale to make a fine point of the distinction between 'hostile intent' and 'hostile act'. Of course, within the twelve-mile limit no such distinction was necessary because the commitment to self-defence was, as in Korea, a commitment to attack any hostile force or its logistics, whether quiescent at the time or not. The 'gunline' established on the coast for naval gunfire support was independent of Operation 'Market Time' and no different in character from the military operations ashore.

The case of the Indo-Pakistan War affords an interesting contrast. The naval operations conducted by India against the port of Karachi and in the Gulf of Bengal took no account of international law, which was, indeed, deliberately put to one side by the Indian naval staff. The result was that the operations spilled over into the high seas, a naval blockade of Pakistan was proclaimed, and shipping was attacked. In the course of these operations neutral ships were sunk, one with total loss of life. In every sense, the Indian naval operations accepted no limitation as to area or scale. Was this, then, a case of 'limited war'?

The important thing to recall about this conflict is that it was so short-lived – about a week. The inconvenience to the international community in that time was not apparent, and there was no time nor occasion for reaction. Had the naval blockade been prolonged and strictly enforced, however, the situation might have become very different, especially if the important tanker traffic through the Straits of Homuz had been incommoded. And despite the short time that the operation was conducted it gave rise subsequently to diplomatic complications. While most shipowners who suffered loss recovered from the insurance brokers under war risks clauses and shrugged their shoulders, the case of a Spanish ship was taken up by the Spanish Government, which demanded compensation from the Indian Government. This was refused.

Whether the Spanish case was put upon the basis that the sinking was illegal because this was not a legal 'war', however it might be designated, or upon the basis of neutrality, might or might not make a difference depending upon the circumstances, for obviously the requirements to avoid damage to neutrals is stricter in the case of actions taken in self-defence than in the case of belligerent operations in conditions of formal and declared war. But, either way, an important point has been demonstrated by the Indo-Pakistan War, and that is the need to conserve the concept of neutrality, and law concerning it, which has generally been overlooked with the demise of the concept of legal war.

The Indo-Pakistan War of 1971 is abnormal also in respect of the immediate and indiscriminate resort to the higher categories of weaponry. Styx missiles were used in the initial engagement, and the operations were conducted from the outset at the highest level. The only comparable case has been that of the Middle East War of 1973, when missile exchanges occurred, although they were in that instance confined to coastal waters. From these two episodes it may be inferred that when full-scale fighting erupts, at sea as well as on land, those who have missiles will use them. In what sense, then, is there a concept of limited war at sea with respect to the modes and scale of weaponry, as distinct from the areas of operation?

Again it is the principle of self-defence that governs the answer. If the conflict is conducted without restraints on weaponry, the scale of response is not disproportionate, nor unnecessary, even if it is at the highest levels. In the two conflicts mentioned that has been the situation from the outbreak of hostilities. But if the situation is different, if an 'armed attack' is of a low order, the mode and scale of weaponry in response is a factor of necessity and proportionality. Most of the occasions of the use of force at sea since 1945 have been of this latter type.

The concept of proportion is the political and legal aspect of the tactical concept of graduated force. If the political goal is severely limited, as in the case of most disputes over natural resources it will be, and if it is necessary to put oneself in a plausible condition of self-defence in the eyes of the United Nations and world opinion, instantaneous resort to the higher and more lethal modes of weaponry will be ruled out, and a subtle game of escalation must be played by naval planners.

In such restricted situations the role of the navy is to exercise influence, by presence and veiled threat if that suffices, by coercion under the claim or pretext of law enforcement if it is not. The side which opens fire first is likely to lose the political advantage of plausibly invoking self-defence, and so the game requires that the other side takes that initial step. So from harassment to collision, to low-level gunfire, to high-level gunfire, and to missiles, provides a logical ladder of the resort to force, the rungs of which will be climbed alternately by the parties to the dispute. The 'Battle of the Paracels' between the Chinese and South Vietnamese navies in 1974 followed just this pattern, with both sides invoking self-defence in the resulting diplomatic exchanges.

In a dispute over fisheries, for example, it would not be necessary or proportionate to resort to missiles when a Bofors gun would suffice to defend what one claims to be a right. But if a Bofors gun is met by a six-inch salvo the response need not be confined to that level, and could take the form of a resort to missiles. The doctrine of graduated escalation fits the legal and political requirements of vindication of national interest.

The types of warships which were available until quite recently provided such tactical means of flexible response, but they are disappearing and being replaced by warships that have no such flexibility. Patrol boats or frigates armed only with missiles are designed for unrestricted combat and have no capacity for low-level coercion. That means either that their presence is without influence, because, like submarines, they lack credibility in coercive situations; or that they amount to a grave threat which can be met only by instantaneous resort to the highest modes of weaponry. Graduated response being impossible, the political as well as the tactical options are closed.

The result, apart from posing new dangers to peace, is that changes are likely to be forced upon us in the concept of limited war at sea and the way it is conducted. It becomes more and more difficult to envisage limited war at sea when it can only be fought in a totally unrestrained way. It is paradoxical that the Russian navy is becoming the only one with ships which have the whole range of weaponry suited to graduated response. (Certainly, the small, newer navies of the Third World, with their missile-carrying patrol boats, stand at the other end of the scale.) What does this portend? Does it mean that the presence of a *Kresta* class is influential in a way that a *Leander* class with guns replaced by Exocet missiles is not, because it represents a credible threat at all possible levels? If a *Kresta* enforces 'visit and search' of British merchant ships by threat of gunfire, does the *Leander* resist by resort to Exocet? It is obvious that the draftsman of rules of engagement for situations of tension has a problem more acute than in the days of six-inch cruisers.

There are other sorts of naval weapons whose appropriateness for limited war is also a matter for discussion. Mine warfare is one of these. It is interesting that this has not been resorted to since 1945 except on the occasion of the mining of Haiphong harbour in May 1972. There are many reasons for this: The inconvenience to international shipping, and the danger of drawing the international community into the conflict in an undesirable way, is one obvious reason. A practical reason is that very few navies have the skill to engage in mine-warfare, or in counter-mine measures, and are shy of the unknown: Third-World countries like prestigious missiles which are known to pack a lethal punch and can be displayed, and find no joy in clandestine ways. But mine-warfare remains one of the most potent means of waging warfare, and in its modern forms is more effective and significant than is generally known. For this reason its use in limited warfare, now that such warfare is likely to be conducted by exchanges of missiles, is bound to give rise to study.

The case of the mining of Haiphong could well prove to be a significant precedent, both for the political and legal aspects of the matter, and the strategic and tactical advantages it offers. The mining of Haiphong was discussed in the early stages of Operation 'Sea Dragon', and it was ruled out in the circumstances then prevailing. Tactical studies based upon mining by aircraft during the Second World War suggested that losses of minelaying aircraft would be disproportionate to gains. The threat to Russian, Polish, and other shipping using Haiphong might have added new complications to the war: it is a fact that North Vietnam was not supplied with surface-to-surface missiles that could have hustled the Seventh Fleet out of the Gulf of Tonkin; it is a fact that the United States did not prevent the supply of North Vietnam by mining Haiphong.

Whatever the tactical and political considerations that caused the United States in 1968 to decide against the mining of Haiphong, the matter was put in a legal context by the suggestion that mining would not be necessary and proportionate in an operation whose rationale was the collective self-defence of South Vietnam. That was how it was put by the occupant of the International Law desk in the Navy Department in the Pentagon, who went on record on the subject in the Judge Advocate General's Journal.[1] No doubt this reassured the Russians when they read it a week later that the United States had put aside the policy of mine-warfare.

But four years later the policy changed, and a highly successful mining operation was conducted. No question of necessity and proportionality now arose. What had occurred to change the policy and the doctrine? The answer is that a complete change of circumstances had occurred. Negotiations to end the war were in an advanced stage, and sensitive pressure had to be put on Hanoi to conclude a deal which the Soviet Union no doubt by now wanted as much as the United States. The pressure was very successful, but so, significantly, was the tactic. There was no loss of minelaying aircraft; the delay in activating the mines, plus full publication of the time delay, enabled a large proportion of shipping to clear Haiphong, and the rest were bottled up. Supplies were cut, and the fact that the United States alone had the know-how and facilities to clear the minefield was a factor in forcing North Vietnam into a settlement. The lessons of Haiphong are not likely to be overlooked.

It is obvious that changing weaponry is forcing changes upon us in the concept of limited war at sea. Conflicts in future will be more difficult to keep under constraint than in the past, and in that sense limited war is likely to be unlimited. In what sense, then, will it remain limited? Probably it will remain limited in area, although this cannot be guaranteed, and there are reasons to suppose that tension will lead to confrontation in the distant waters of the Cape route. It will remain limited in goal since, at least in this generation, the disposition to subjugate is not evident, and even the Kremlin seeks influence by proxy rather than by direct coercion. So for the foreseeable future the factor common to all cases of resort to naval force will be invocation of the rules of self-defence. That is what justifies an academic study of the concept of limited war at sea.

The beneficiaries of this study are the naval staffs who have to draft the rules of engagement (which authorize the use of fire) and operational orders. Theirs is a difficult task because they have to envisage the political circumstances under which they will be authorized to order the use of force, and they have to comprehend the legal concepts under which the politicians can justify it. Limited war implies limitations as to operational areas and operational conduct. Even if no limitation is put upon the level of force to be used, the fact that the operational goal is limited will require specification in the rules of engagement which in the Second World War were unnecessary and not envisaged. The intellectual framework of limited war has thus become an essential component of the professional activity of naval staffs.

NOTES

1. Captain F. E. Carlisle, 'The Interrelationship of international law and U.S. naval operations in South-East Asia', *J.A.G. Journal of U.S. Navy*, 22 (1967), p. 11.

8

WARS OF NATIONAL LIBERATION AND WAR CRIMINALITY

G. I. A. D. Draper

a: The Background:

The classical law of war has bequeathed to us a fundamental distinction between *jus ad bellum* and *jus in bello*, the former dealing with recourse to war and the latter with conduct in warfare. This distinction took some time to emerge. It was impeded in the medieval period by the theological–legal doctrine of the 'just war'. Under this doctrine the major emphasis was laid upon the authority of the Prince, the 'justness' of the 'cause' for which there had been resort to war and the 'right intention' of the individual participants. Much less emphasis was laid upon the manner in which hostilities were conducted. The *jus in bello*, at that period styled the *jus militare*, had a more secular and professional base being derived in large part from the usages of the knights and the professional military classes. This *jus militare* was confined to those who followed the military calling and was an amalgam of rules of honourable conduct for the members of the knightly orders of chivalry, and strict practices controlling such important matters as claims to ransoms and spoils. Those who were outside the military classes did not benefit from the *jus militare*, being devoid of honour and not entitled to ransom and spoils.[1]

Warfare directed against women and children, religious and clerks was not considered 'a just war'. Moreover total war, as we call it today, could not be 'just'. In the main the 'just war' idea, inherited from the *jus fetiale* of the early Roman law and introduced into the Christian ethic by St. Augustine and refined by St. Thomas Aquinas, had little to say about the conduct of warfare. It certainly was not a restraining factor. Between the knightly and professional military classes the *jus militare* applied. Conduct such as perfidy was prohibited. The strict and technical rules regarding title to ransom and spoils restricted military excesses and limited legitimate participation in warfare. The loss of honour and of title to ransom were serious matters, but humanitarian restraints had no place.[2]

A serious consequence derived from the 'just war' idea was that both belligerents could not be waging a just war. God was behind the just cause. The adversary was not in like case. God's will was not then, and probably is not now, divisible.[3] Princes were not in the habit of admitting that wars 'avowed' by them were other than just. A later development of the 'just war' idea was a combination of the theological and judicial. The judgement of God was seen in the fact of victory. The 'just' Prince was punishing the 'unjust' adversary on God's behalf, in this world, as the devils in hell would punish the defeated in the next. By the late fourteenth century the moral content of the 'just war' idea receded, to be replaced by the idea of a 'public and open' war conducted exclusively by knights and the military professionals on behalf of a Prince. This excluded both the feudal foray or 'private war' and the notorious 'freebooters' whose actions were seen as outside the limits of lawful warfare and as acts of brigandage for which they might be summarily executed when caught.[4]

The just war idea lingered long and delayed the acceptance of the principle that the law of war bound both belligerents alike. Grotius can take much of the credit for formulating this important principle in his work, *De jure belli ac Pacis* written in the years 1623–4. He insisted that the law of war should be observed by both belligerents irrespective of the just or unjust nature of their cause. He included in this work his *temperamenta belli* which came to be the foundations of much of the customary law of war of the seventeenth and eighteenth centuries.[5]

By the second half of the nineteenth century legal positivism was in full sway and the older ideas of natural law and the 'just war' were in retreat. As part of the positivist movement in international law the end of the century saw the precocious and extensive codification of the customary law of war. At the Hague Peace Conferences of 1899 and 1907, thirteen international conventions were established, dealing with the law of war on land, at sea, neutrality and, more modestly, the pacific settlement of disputes. It has been said that pure positivism is a contradiction in terms. A new and secular set of values permeated the content of this codified law of war, namely, the humanitarian ideals, pioneered by such men as Dunant, Lieber, and de Martens, the academic jurist adviser of Tsar Nicholas II at the two Hague Peace Conferences.[6] This precocious codification of the law of war, the first part of international law to receive that treatment, had a price. The law of war became, certainly, by the mid-twentieth century, a major anachronism of international law. Yet the nineteenth-century codification was carried out on the firm premise that the law of war applied without regard to the 'cause' of the belligerent's resort to war. The humanitarian nature of the codified law of war can be seen in the famous de Martens preamble to Hague Convention No IV of 1907, dealing with the Law and Customs of War on land:

These provisions the drafting of which has been inspired by the desire to diminish the evils of war, so far as military requirements permit, are intended to serve as a general rule of conduct for the belligerents in their mutual relations and in relation to the inhabitants . . . In cases not covered by the rules adopted . . . the inhabitants and the belligerents remain under the protection . . . of the principles of the law of nations, derived from the usages established among civilized peoples, from the laws of humanity and the dictates of the public conscience.

This development was accompanied by another, namely, the high tide of state sovereignty. Thereby, States were entitled to resort to war as an instrument of national policy, i.e. as an exercise of their sovereignty. This inherent right might be curtailed solely by the conclusion of a treaty. Hall, a leading English jurist of the period, writing in 1880, expressed the legal position in a famous passage:

International law has no alternative but to accept war, independently of the justice of its origin, as a relation which the parties to it may set up, if they choose, and to busy itself only in regulating the effects of the relation. Hence both parties to every war are regarded as being in an identical legal position, and consequently as being possessed of equal rights.[7]

Since the end of the First World War we have witnessed a major departure from 'the sovereign right' idea and a return to a severely restricted legal right of States to resort to war. Thus in 1920 we had the restrictions imposed by the Covenant of the League of Nations whereby a State might not resort to war until a limited period of time had elapsed after the failure of pacific means of settlement of dispute.[8] In the Pact of Paris of 1928 we had the renunciation of war as 'an instrument of national policy' and an obligation to settle disputes pacifically, with a reservation of the right of self-defence.[9] In 1945 we had the wide prohibition in Article 2 (4) of the Charter of the U.N. whereby Members were forbidden to use, or threaten, force against any State except under the auspices of the U.N. or in self-defence. More recently, and less authoritatively, there has been the Definition of Aggression adopted by the U.N. General Assembly in 1974.[10]

In the light of these developments and the condemnation of the defendant at the Nuremberg International Military Tribunal for planning and waging aggressive war, it is not entirely surprising that attempts have been made to resurrect and agitate the question whether illegal resort to war should carry with it the full benefits of the law of war, i.e. the *jus in bello*. If aggressive war were the major war crime under cover of which all other war crimes, including genocide, took place, then how can the law of war apply with equal and impartial effect upon the aggressor and the victim, at least so far as the benefits of such law are concerned? Some urged a rejection of the right of neutrality in relation to the aggressor. Others urged that the substantial benefits of the law governing military occupation of enemy territory should be likewise denied.[11] Until now the modern law of war has resisted such claims, not without much heart-searching among jurists. The argument in favour of resistance to such claims has been put by one jurist thus:

the laws of war are binding on all participants in hostilities not because of any presumed equality of right between the belligerents irrespective of the legality or illegality of their recourse to force, but because any recourse to force, whether legal or illegal, remains subject to the restrictions of the laws of war on overriding grounds of policy and humanity.[12]

Thereby, it is contended, the *hereditas damnosa* of the 'just war' doctrine, with all the slaughter and cruelties that attended it, might be avoided.

Both the Hague Conventions of 1907 and the present

Geneva Conventions of 1949[13] are imbued with humanitarian principles, and reject any idea of their unequal application based upon the legality or illegality of the 'cause' for which the belligerents have resorted to armed conflict. In the former instrument, this was made clear by the de Martens preamble cited above. In the latter Article 1, common to each of the four Conventions, provides: 'The High Contracting Parties undertake to respect and to ensure respect for the Convention in all circumstances.' The Geneva Conventions of 1949 now bind 143 States.[14] They deal with the protection of war victims in international armed conflicts. The First Convention deals with the protection of Service sick and wounded, the Second with Service sick, wounded, and shipwrecked at sea, the Third with prisoners of war, and the Fourth with civilians in enemy territory or in territory occupied by the enemy. They comprise in all 417 detailed Articles and represent a substantial part of what is now known as the International Humanitarian Law of Armed Conflicts. The principle of non-discrimination of application is central to all these four instruments, as it is in the contemporary instruments relating to Human Rights Law,[15] to which they are allied, in legal theory.

There has been during the last decade a modified recrudescence of the idea that the 'cause' for which an armed struggle has been initiated by one participant ought to determine whether such struggle is an international armed conflict to which the modern *jus in bello* i.e. the Humanitarian Law of Armed Conflicts, is applicable. This movement is, upon analysis, not towards a discrimination in the application of that law of armed conflict. It is a move for a discriminatory basis upon which struggles for selective 'causes' should be considered as international armed conflicts. It is, in effect, a double discrimination, as to the identity of a new belligerent 'entity', and as to the 'cause' for which it resorts to armed force. It is this development which now calls for consideration, in the light of recent law-making developments relating to armed conflicts.

b: Self-Determination and Belligerent Participation:

The Hague Conventions of 1907 and the Geneva Conventions

of 1949 were redacted on the basis that they applied
exclusively to inter-State armed conflicts. Consistent with that
approach they limited belligerent status to the armed forces of
States, with a modest extension to volunteer corps and militia,
in 1907, and to organized resistence movements operating
within or without occupied territory, in 1949.[16] All such
armed groups had to belong to or depend upon a Party to the
conflict, namely, a State. The most extreme concession was a
levée en masse, legally defined as 'inhabitants of a non-occupied
territory who on the approach of the enemy spontaneously
take up arms to resist the invading forces, without having had
time to form themselves into regular armed units'.[17] Comba-
tancy was extended to such volunteer units, organized
resistance movements and *levées en masse* on specific and
stringent conditions. These conditions had been imposed in
1907 for combatants, and were repeated for P.O.W. status in
the Geneva (P.O.W.) Convention of 1949. Such combatants
had to: (i) be under responsible command; (ii) wear a
distinctive and discernible sign; (iii) carry their arms openly;
and (iv) conduct their operations in accordance with the law
of war. Members of *levées en masse* were required to meet only
the last two conditions. No relaxation of these conditions was
made in deference to the 'cause' for which the State upon
which such combatants depended had resorted to armed force.
Article 1 of the Regulations annexed to Hague Convention
No IV of 1907 conferred combatant status upon such persons.
Article 4 A (2) of the Geneva (P.O.W.) Convention of 1949
conferred prisoner of war status upon them 'when they fell
into the power of the enemy'. The sole extension made in 1949
was in favour of 'organized resistance movements, operating
in or out of occupied territory'. This was based upon the
experience of the Second World War. Such extensions of
combatant and P.O.W. status in no way deflected the exclusive
application of the Hague Convention No IV of 1907 and the
Geneva Conventions of 1949 to States. Such combatants were
required to depend upon States. The conflicts to which those
instruments applied were inter-State armed conflicts.

International law approached the resort to, and control of,
internal armed conflicts, i.e. armed rebellions, in a different

manner. Each State had, as part of its inherent sovereignty, the right to quell armed rebellion within its territory, but rebellion was not the concern, let alone a violation of, international law. Full-scale civil wars, with recognition of belligerency accorded to the rebel party by the government of the State concerned or by third States, somewhat rare events, were governed, as to the manner in which they were conducted, by the customary law of war. In the absence of such recognition of belligerency the manner of armed response to the rebellion was left to the sovereign discretion of the government concerned. This would be a matter for the internal penal law as to emergency and treason. Generally it would be licit to use the amount and kind of armed force necessary to quell the rebellion. However, for the first time, in the Geneva Conventions of 1949, there was contained a common Article 3 limited solely to armed conflicts not of an international character occurring in the territory of a State party to those instruments. This Article set out the basic humanitarian prohibitions binding alike on government and rebel forces, being a microcosm of the remainder of those Conventions governing international, i.e. inter-State armed conflicts.

The Geneva Conventions of 1949 are primarily backwards-looking to the experiences of the Second World War. They deal with the humanitarian treatment of service personnel and civilians in the hands of the enemy, known as 'war victims', as opposed to the conduct of military operations. Excellent in their own area, the Conventions in no way sought to control, except to a vestigial degree, military operations, targetry, and the use of weapons. The rules governing military operations and the use of weapons on land rested as they had been codified by the Hague Convention No IV of 1907, with certain minor exceptions. By the mid-twentieth century the anachronisms of this part of the law of war were readily apparent.

The common Article 3 proved inadequate to restrain the conduct of internal armed conflicts, which were frequent phenomena in the post-1945 era, causing heavy loss of life, great destruction, and hardship to innocent civilians. Neither did it deal with military operations, targetry, or the use of weaponry. Moreover, Governments were not willing to admit that such internal conflicts existed in their territory or to accept, in practice, the basic humanitarian restraints in that one provision. Also, there were a number of 'mixed' armed conflicts in which the armed forces of third States participated on one or on both sides of an internal armed conflict. The law of war applicable in such situations was not clear or easy to apply. The divisive political and racial ideologies of the post-1945 era have accentuated the number and intensity of such 'mixed' conflicts.

The International Committee of the Red Cross (I.C.R.C.), the custodian of the Humanitarian Law of Armed Conflicts, who had been the initiators of the series of Geneva Conventions from 1864 to 1949, have taken new steps to try to secure a major revision of the existing law of armed conflicts, both international and internal, to meet the admittedly unsatisfactory and imbalanced condition of the contemporary law of war. After a false start in the period 1956–8,[18] the I.C.R.C. launched, in 1971, an ambitious project for modernizing, revising and elaborating Hague Convention No IV of 1907 dealing with conduct in land hostilities, particularly for the protection of civilians from their effects and for extending the humanitarian protection of the four Geneva Conventions of 1949 to wider classes of war victims, particularly civilians not protected by those instruments. In the main, the major purpose of this redaction can now be seen as the making of new legal rules for the protection to civilians from the effects of modern land hostilities, particularly from the indiscriminative and destructive effects of modern weaponry. This major undertaking sought both to reaffirm and extend and exploit the implicit and fundamental rule of the law of war that civilians should not be the subject of deliberate attack and that the means of civilian existence should not be destroyed in hostilities. Ancillary to this purpose was the extension and amplification of the humanitarian treatment to be accorded to extended classes of civilians who find themselves in the hands of the adversary in time of armed conflict. Yet a third purpose was to overtake, without superseding, Article 3 common to the

Conventions of 1949, and to frame a separate instrument confined exclusively to internal armed conflicts which should echo as much as possible the parallel instrument designed to govern international armed conflicts on the lines indicated.

In the years 1971–3 the I.C.R.C. convoked meetings of Government Experts at Geneva to prepare the draft texts of two 'Protocols additional to the Geneva Conventions of 1949'. These were to be submitted to a Diplomatic Conference of States, convened by the Swiss Federal Council with a view to establishing the two Protocols. Protocol 1 was to be devoted to international armed conflicts and Protocol 2 to internal conflicts.[19]

A collateral but powerful impetus to this law-making movement came from the General Assembly of the U.N. in a series of resolutions adopted under the rubric 'Respect for Human Rights in Armed Conflict', the most recent of which was adopted in January 1977. These resolutions, adopted normally by consensus, displayed the support of the international community for the establishment of the two Protocols. They also displayed the close nexus, in juridical terms, between the international law regimes of Human Rights and the new Humanitarian Law of Armed Conflicts, particularly in relation to the proposed Protocol 2 dealing exclusively with internal conflicts. The law of war is concerned with the relationship between belligerents. The law of Human Rights is concerned with the relationship between the governed and the Governments. The law governing internal armed conflicts is necessarily concerned with both.

By 1974 the draft texts of the two Protocols were ready for submission to the Diplomatic Conference on the Reaffirmation and Development of International Humanitarian Law applicable in armed conflicts, convened by the Swiss Federal Council. This Conference held four sessions, one in each of the years 1974–7, in Geneva. Of the 166 States invited, 124 attended the first session (1974), 120 the second (1975), 107 the third (1976), and 109 the fourth and last (1977). Eleven National Liberation movements (N.L.M.s), recognized by regional organizations of States, and 51 inter-governmental and non-governmental organizations also attended, making a total of some 700 delegates.[20] Only Government delegates had the right to vote.

The Final Act of the Conference was signed on 10 June 1977, by 102 States and 3 N.L.M.s. This Final Act authenticated and recorded the texts of the two Protocols adopted by consensus in the final plenary session of the Conference in 1977.[21] Both instruments are styled 'Protocols Additional to the Geneva Conventions of 1949', Protocol 1 relating to international, and Protocol 2 to internal, armed conflicts. These instruments were open to signature and accession of States from 12 December 1977. They come into force six months after two States have ratified or acceded to them. Thereafter, for each State ratifying or acceding, they come in force six months after the deposit with the depositary (Switzerland) of its instrument of ratification or accession.[22] Protocol 1 contains 102 Articles and Protocol 2 contains 28. In fact, Protocol 1 is additional not only to the Conventions of 1949 but also to those Parts of Hague Conventions No IV of 1907 which deal with the conduct of hostilities. Thus for the first time since 1907 that part of the law of war dealing with hostilities is to be found in the same instrument with that dealing with the treatment of war-victims in the hands of the enemy. There has been, therefore, a modified merger of the 'Hague' and 'Geneva' streams of law. This merger has its echo, on a restricted basis, in Protocol 2. Now, for the first time, there is an instrument of international law dealing exclusively with internal armed conflicts.

Protocol 1 deals with a wide range of topics, the chief of which are: (i) protection of the civilian wounded, sick and shipwrecked, medical installations and transport on land, sea and in the air; (ii) combatant and P.O.W. status for irregular fighters; (iii) the conduct of hostilities; (iv) military objectives; (v) the like protection of civilian objects, habitat, and means of existence, of the environment and of installations containing dangerous forces; (vi) protection of civilians in enemy hands; (vii) the appointment and functioning of Protecting Powers and substitute organizations; and (viii) the repression of 'grave breaches' of the Protocol.

The Conventions of 1949 defined their scope in a common

Article 2, which set out the situations to which they applied. Those situations were inter-state armed conflicts in which the belligerents were States Parties to the Conventions. At the first session of the Diplomatic Conference in 1974, a corresponding scope Article, 1, in Protocol 1 fell for consideration. This orthodox proposal encountered, head on, another proposal arising from a development which had been taking place in the U.N. and in the U.N. Human Rights regimes. This proposal transcended and traversed the existing dichotomy between international and internal armed conflicts on which the scheme of the Conventions of 1949 and of the two Protocols presented to the Conference then rested. This was the movement, already accomplished in Article 1 of the two U.N. International Covenants on Human Rights of 1966, to transform 'the principle of self-determination of peoples', set out as a Purpose of the U.N. in Article 1 (1) of the U.N. Charter, into a fundamental Human Right, as exemplified in Article 1 of the U.N. Covenant on Civil and Political Rights, 1966. The 'principle of self-determination of peoples' played an important part in the process of decolonization as can be seen in the U.N. Declaration on the Granting of Independence to Colonial Countries and Peoples, 1960, adopted in resolution 1514 (XIV).[23] This Declaration condemned 'the subjection of peoples to alien subjugation, domination and exploitation' as a denial of fundamental human rights, as contrary to the U.N. Charter and an impediment to world peace. This thinking was given legal formulation in Article 1 of the U.N. Covenant on Civil and Political Rights, 1966, whereby: 'All peoples have the right of self-determination. By virtue of that right they freely determine their political status . . .' The matter was further advanced in the U.N. Declaration on 'Principles of International Law concerning Friendly Relations and Co-operation among . . . States', adopted by consensus in the General Assembly in October 1970.[24] The Fourth Principle of that Declaration, after repeating that the subjection of peoples to alien subjugation was a violation of the principle of self-determination and a denial of fundamental human rights, was elaborated in these terms: 'Every State has the duty to refrain from any forcible action which deprives peoples referred to above in the elaboration of the present Principle of their right to self-determination and independence.'

The conjunction of this development from the *principle*, to a fundamental human *right*, of self-determination of peoples and the correlative prohibition of States using force to deprive peoples of that right, reiterated in subsequent U.N. resolutions, was seen by a large number of States to have a direct relevance to the new Humanitarian Law of Armed Conflicts envisaged in the two Protocols additional to the Conventions of 1949. To such States that relevance was an imperative in political terms whatever might be the juridical dislocation caused to the new Protocols. It soon became apparent in the first session of the Conference that there would be a majority for any proposal that struggles by peoples against colonial, alien, or racist domination be treated as international conflicts, for the purposes of Protocol 1, and not as internal conflicts, for the purposes of Protocol 2. The Third World States were not slow to see that a major political and a possible juridical advantage might be obtained, at one move, by securing the insertion of a provision in the scope Article, 1, of Protocol 1 whereby the struggles of peoples against colonial, alien, and racist regimes should be included as situations to which the Conventions of 1949 and Protocol 1 would be applicable. By orthodox legal thinking such struggles were internal armed conflicts to which the Article 3, common to the Conventions of 1949 and Protocol 2 might be applicable. Once such 'peoples' struggles' for the selective purposes mentioned were ingested within the scope of Protocol 1, they assuredly had no place in Protocol 2. The two Protocols had been drafted on the basis of mutual exclusion.[25] for the National Liberation Movements and the Governments which supported them and who commanded the majority of votes, this was a political objective as manifest as it was desirable.

Accordingly, at the first session in 1974, a provision, Article 1 (4) of Protocol 1, was adopted which specified that the situations to which the Protocol applies included: 'armed conflicts in which peoples are fighting against colonial domination and alien occupation and against racist régimes in the exercise of their right of self-determination, as enshrined in the Charter of the United Nations . . . and the Declaration on Principles of International Law' (1970).

The vote in the relevant Committee (1) which adopted this insertion was 70–21–13, considerably less than the support obtained for the Principles of self-determination of peoples in the Declaration on Principles of International Law in the U.N. General Assembly in 1970.[26] The States which were the latent targets of what may be styled the 'N.L.M. insertion' in Protocol 1, were Israel, Portugal, and South Africa. Portugal, by an internal change of the Metropolitan government, dissolved its colonial nexus. The N.L.M.s in two former Portuguese colonies became the Governments of two new States, Mozambique and Angola. South Africa declined to attend the Conference after the first session in 1974, but Israel remained until the end.

The precise juridical effects of the inclusion of N.L.M. struggles within the scope of Protocol 1 has not yet been fully assessed. As that instrument, like the Conventions of 1949 which it supplements, has been framed on the premise that it applies solely to inter-State armed conflicts, these effects cannot be minimal. Moreover, it would appear that there has been an addition to the law governing the resort to armed force, the *jus ad bellum*, beyond the limits in Article 2 (4) of the U.N. Charter. It is, in effect, a twofold addition. First, it adds to the 'entities' which have the lawful competence to engage in international armed conflicts. Second, the criteria for such entities are based exclusively upon the 'cause' for which they 'struggle'. These 'causes' are racial, and hence wholly discriminatory in nature. Discrimination is expressly repugnant to the Humanitarian Law of Armed Conflicts as well as to the regimes of Human Rights. Thus we have the paradoxical situation that discriminatory 'causes' have afforded the route by which the benefit of the law of war, which rejects discrimination, has been made applicable to those resorting to armed force for such 'causes'. Thus discrimination, *ratione personae et causae*, and that fatal conflux of *jus ad bellum* and *jus in bello*, have been achieved at one fell swoop.

Occupation of enemy territories, the conduct of hostilities, the appointment and functioning of Protecting Powers, the penal repression of 'grave breaches' and other topics governed by the Conventions and Protocol 1 present major difficulties when applicable to N.L.M.s.

The effect on the innovatory Protocol 2 is also marked. This instrument contained a scope provision, Article 1, which did not fall for debate until the second session of the Conference in 1975. One manifest type of internal conflict under the classical law of war, namely, struggles for self-determination by peoples, had been excluded from its ambit by its express inclusion in Protocol 1. This did little to add to the appeal of Protocol 2 to the newer States, on account of the fragility of their Governments, and to older States where revolutions are not rare events. A Government of a newly seceded State or a revolutionary Government in an existing State, is not eager to subscribe to an instrument which inhibits the methods it adopts for quelling an armed rebellion. Moreover, Protocol 2 contains detailed humanitarian prohibitions designed to secure humane treatment for those persons whose liberty is restricted or who are otherwise affected by the internal conflict. Protocol 2 came before the Conference with 48 Articles, and was framed to echo the salient provisions in Protocol 1. As authenticated and adopted at the signing of the Final Act of the Conference in June 1977 it contains but 28 Articles. The reason is clear. A much reduced and debilitated Protocol 2 was the price of its survival. This process of reduction took place in somewhat hurried and confused conditions in the final phases of the Conference in 1977. It may be said that its adoption was more of a gesture by States than a solid and genuine addition to the Humanitarian Law governing internal armed conflicts. Such conflicts are frequently marked by great lack of restraint, and by gross inhumanity.

Nevertheless, something concrete was achieved. The scope provision of Protocol 2, Article 1, has particular relevance to, and illuminates the impact of, the 'N.L.M. insertion' in Article 1 (4) (the scope provision), of Protocol 1. Part of the difficulty with Article 3, common to the four Conventions of 1949, had been the uncertainty of its application, particularly on the level of intensity of the armed conflict requisite to bring

Article 3 to bear. Protocol 2 sought to avoid that uncertainty. There was much debate on this topic at the second session, in 1975. In the end the 'high level' school won the day. In political terms, a 'high level' conflict, proximate to the classical civil-war situation, was more palatable. It reduced artificiality, limited the scope of the Protocol, and reflected the proximate nature of the two Protocols. An internal conflict, governed by detailed rules borrowed from those applicable to inter-State armed conflicts, requires participants to be so organized as to be able to comply with those rules, if the traditional and mischievous propensity of the law of war to artificiality[27] is to be avoided. Article 1 of Protocol 2, the scope provisions, was accordingly framed and adopted thus:

1. This Protocol, which develops and supplements Article 3 common to the ... Conventions ... of 1949 without modifying its existing conditions of application, shall apply to all armed conflicts not covered by Article 1 of (Protocol 1) and which take place in the territory of a High Contracting Party between its armed forces and dissident armed forces or other organized armed groups which, under responsible command, exercise such control over a part of its territory as to enable them to carry out sustained and concerted military operations and to implement this Protocol.
2. This Protocol shall not apply to situations of internal disturbances and tensions, such as riots, isolated and sporadic acts of violence and other acts of a similar nature, as not being armed conflicts.

The application of the Protocol has thus been based upon pragmatic and objective criteria. The Protocol applies to armed conflicts between contending parties which are in a position to meet its obligations. It does not apply to fights at football matches, violent demonstrations, or to the 'kill and run' types of armed activity such as have been experienced in Northern Ireland. Such activities are not 'sustained and concerted military operations' however much it may be claimed that 'organized armed groups' are committed. Neither is there the exercise of such control over a part of the State's territory as to enable such dissident armed groups to carry out such sustained and concerted military operations. In the result, Protocol 2, unlike Article 3 common to the Conventions of 1949, has a limited but viable application, namely, to internal armed conflicts proximate to the full scale, classical civil wars such as that in Spain from 1936 to 1939, and in Nigeria in 1969. Manifestly, there is still no lack of situations in which Article 3 is still applicable.

N.L.M. struggles ought, on juridical grounds, to have found a place within Protocol 2, and not in Protocol 1. Nevertheless it can be contended that the rationale behind the scope provision in Article 1 of Protocol 2 is equally cogent and controlling in determining the level of intensity of struggles against alien or racist regimes by peoples in exercise of their right of self determination now within Protocol 1. Such 'peoples' or their authority, must be in a position to fulfil the extensive obligations imposed by that instrument. At the very minimum it may be urged they must have that degree of territorial control, military organization, and discipline as will enable them to carry out sustained and concerted military organizations, as requisite in Protocol 2. If the capacity of such 'peoples' is limited to the 'kill and run' type of activity, their struggle should properly be excluded from the ambit of both Protocols. In their final statements preceding the signing of the Final Act of the Conference in 1977 certain States indicated that they had adopted the text of Protocol 1 on that understanding. Nothing in the Protocols repudiates that interpretation. The inner nature and content of Protocol 1 is consistent with such interpretative statements. If that be the reasonable interpretation of the 'N.L.M. insertion' in Protocol 1, then that insertion accords more satisfactorily with the remaining provisions, or at least with most of them. Thereby the purpose of the instrument is furthered and not frustrated.

In spite of the rejection by the Humanitarian Law of Armed Conflicts of the principle of discrimination,[28] the 'N.L.M. insertion' has obtruded discrimination into Protocol 1. It may perhaps be seen as a vestigial and modified remnant of the old 'just war' theory. The nature of the 'cause' for which an entity resorted to armed force, may, by selective criteria, e.g. race, convert that entity to a lawful participant in international armed conflicts. In legal theory the difficulties are formidable. In practice, the humanitarian *jus in bello* may still operate effectively on the Grotian principle that the 'just' or 'unjust' nature of the resort to armed conflict should in no way affect

the impartial application of the law governing that conflict.[29]
Protocol I does not enable an N.L.M. to be a Party to that
instrument.[30] Signing the Final Act of a Conference is quite a
distinct matter from being a Party to the instrument
authenticated and adopted in that Final Act. A special
mechanism has been devised, in Article 96 (3) of Protocol I,
whereby in an armed conflict in which an N.L.M. is engaged:

The authority representing a people engaged against a High Contracting
Party in an armed conflict . . . may undertake to apply the Conventions and
this Protocol in relation to the conflict by means of a declaration addressed
to the depositary (Switzerland). Such declaration shall upon receipt by the
depositary have in relation to that conflict the following effects:

(a) the Conventions and this Protocol are brought into force for the said
authority as a Party to the conflict with immediate effect;
(b) the said authority assumes the same rights and obligation as those
which have been assumed by the High Contracting Party to the
Conventions and this Protocol; and
(c) the Conventions and this Protocol are equally binding upon all
Parties to the conflict.

This mechanism, and its effects, make clear that however
discriminatory may be the 'cause' for which the N.L.M. has
become a Party to the conflict, the full benefit and burden of
the Conventions and of the Protocol, i.e. humanitarian *jus in
bello*, applies equally to the N.L.M. and its adversary. The
element of discrimination, if not removed from the *jus ad
bellum*, has been reduced in the area where it is most likely to
weaken the law applicable, the *jus in bello*.

What is not made explicit in the Protocol is the situation in
which the N.L.M. fails or declines to make such a declaration
under Article 96 (3). It would seem that not being Parties to
the Protocol they have not taken the requisite steps under that
Protocol to make it applicable to them as a Party to the
Conflict. The scope provision, Article 1 (4), does not get over
that failure for that provision controls application of the whole
Protocol, including Article 96 (3) as to declarations.

c : The new war criminality:

It cannot be denied that the full application of the benefit and
burdens of Protocol I to N.L.M.s poses a number of legal and
practical difficulties. Thus the proper functioning of the

Protecting Power system under the Conventions and the Protocol will rarely be possible. Humanitarian Law instruments expressly require monitoring and supervision for their effective implementation. In inter-State armed conflicts this has proved difficult in the past. The Soviet States have rejected the system as inimical to their sovereignty.[31] I.C.R.C. delegates were never allowed a presence in North Korea, North Vietnam, or in the People's Republic of China. With N.L.M.s the situation has all the difficulties inherent in seeking to monitor what is in reality an internal conflict, a situation in which the Protecting Power system does not operate. The enforcement of the Conventions of 1949 and Protocol 1 which supplements them (Article 1 (3)) relies heavily upon a system of penal repression of 'grave breaches' by the legislative and judicial apparatus of States. The older system of resort to reprisals has virtually been eliminated from the Humanitarian Law of Armed Conflicts except in limited areas of battle conduct. Reprisals and humanitarian law are in discord. Resort to reprisals against war victims had already been prohibited by the Coventions of 1949. Likewise, reprisals have been prohibited in Protocol 1 in relation to attacks against civilians, civilian objects, habitat, and means of existence, the environment, cultural objects and places of worship, and installations containing dangerous forces.[32] A possible vestigial lawful resort to reprisals may be the use of illegal weapons against enemy forces and military targets.

This virtual removal of reprisals from the modalities of the humanitarian law of war available for its enforcement has thrown a renewed and not entirely welcome emphasis upon the other traditional means of enforcement, namely, the repression of war criminality. The system in the Conventions of 1949,[33] which has been extended to Protocol 1, by Article 85, is to list certain heinous breaches of the instrument as 'grave breaches'. States undertake (i) to make such acts punishable under their domestic criminal law; (ii) to search for and bring to trial before their own courts any person, irrespective of his nationality, against whom evidence is available that he committed a 'grave breach'; and (iii) alternatively, to hand over such a person to another State that has *prima facie* evidence that the person demanded has committed such an act, in accordance with the law of the State from which rendition is demanded. The Conventions of 1949 did not purport to deal with battle conduct. It followed that 'grave breaches' of that Convention were acts directed against 'protected persons', namely, persons defenceless in the hands of the enemy, such as prisoners of war and civilians in enemy hands or occupied territory. By Article 85 of Protocol 1 this system of repression has been applied to designated 'grave breaches' of the Protocol. Article 85 (3) and (4) lists these 'grave breaches'. They include serious violations of certain of the prohibitions relating to battle conduct, e.g. attacks directed against civilians or indiscriminate attacks affecting civilians. Thus for the first time States may be under an obligation of international law to make such prohibited battle-conduct domestic crimes triable in the ordinary criminal or military courts of a State. To the extent that such acts are not already crimes under the law of a State, legislation must be enacted for that purpose. If a Parliament declines so to enact, the State concerned will not be in a position to ratify the Protocol or not to ratify without a reservation to the relevant Article, 85, of Protocol 1.

This requirement to legislate so as to ingest 'grave breaches' of the Conventions of 1949 into the penal law of the U.K. was the main reason for the delay of eight years between the signing of the Conventions and their ratification by the U.K. Not until the Geneva Conventions Act, 1957, had been enacted was the U.K. in a position to ratify those Conventions later that year. All 'grave breaches' of those instruments are 'arrestable offences' triable by the superior criminal courts of the U.K. The technical difficulties of the draftsman of the Act were more of an obstacle than any division of opinion in either House of Parliament. In fact there was none. In the twenty-seven years that have elapsed since the Geneva Conventions came into force in 1950, no case is known of any person being brought to trial in any State charged with a 'grave breach'. That is not to say that 'grave breaches' have not been committed in that period. If committed by a national, the prosecuting agencies of the State concerned, whether military or civil, normally elect to try such national for the corresponding common crime under the domestic law, e.g. murder or the appropriate form of wounding as the case may be. Lt. Calley of the U.S. Army was tried by U.S. court-martial for the offence of 'murder of a number of unknown Asiatics' in My Lai. There was court-martial jurisdiction for such an offence under the U.S. Uniform Code of Military Justice,[34] the statutory military law of the U.S.A. This removed the trial from the 'grave breaches' provisions of the Convention. More usually the inhibition of the trials of captured enemy personnel for 'grave breaches' has been the fact that a number of service personnel of the State considering trial are detained by the enemy. This negative experience of trials for 'grave breaches' over twenty-seven years did not prevent a number of States at the Diplomatic Conference from seeking to augment the list of 'grave breaches' of the Protocol and, in particular, to include therein a large number of violations of the battle conduct provisions. Prominent in this enthusiasm for judicial repression were the Soviet States. A like enthusiasm was not discernible among the 'Western' and like-minded States. The ultimate compromise is now seen in Article 85 of Protocol 1 adopted at the signing of the Final Act.

States only were parties to the Conventions of 1949, and only such States can be Parties to the Protocols. The operation of the 'grave breaches' system in relation to N.L.M.s has not been explored. It was found sufficiently difficult to reach an agreed text on 'grave breaches' of the Protocol without the added complication of bringing the system to bear in N.L.M. struggles. It is clear that N.L.M.s normally do not have the legislative and judicial apparatus required to meet the stringent requirements of the Conventions and of Protocol 1 as to the trial of person accused of 'grave breaches' of those instruments. The mechanism of declaration of intent to apply these instruments, under Article 96 (3), cannot, it is thought, be used with modifications or reservations. There remains a course of action open to N.L.M.s within, it is thought, the rules governing the repression of 'grave breaches'. An N.L.M. might, if it had *prima facie* evidence of commission, hand over a suspected offender to a neighbouring State which was a Party to the instruments for trial. Here the absence of an N.L.M. legal system will not inhibit the rendition. In the political alignment of N.L.M.s it may not be difficult to find a neighbouring State willing to accept and bring the offender to trial for a 'grave breach' of the Conventions or of Protocol I.

Whether Legislative Assemblies and Parliaments will be prepared to legislate for the punishment of certain 'grave breaches' listed in Protocol is uncertain. Thus Article 85 (3) provides:

the following acts shall be regarded as grave breaches of this Protocol, when committed wilfully, in violation of the relevant provisions of this Protocol, and causing death or serious injury to body or health:

(a) making the civilian population or individual civilians the object of attack;

(b) Launching an indiscriminate attack affecting the civilian population or civilian objects in the knowledge that such attack will cause excessive loss of life, injury to civilians or damage to civilian objects
. . .

The attraction of legislating to make such acts crimes under U.K. law is not enhanced by the fact that reprisal action taken against an enemy for having previously and consistently committed the like acts is forbidden by the Protocol.[35] Such reprisals are therefore a 'grave breach' and therefore have to be criminal under U.K. law. Clearly a fixed penalty is not likely to find a place in any legislation passed to meet the 'grave breach' requirements of the Protocol.

By para. 4 of the same article, 85, a new 'grave breach' was included which may well attract the interest of N.L.M.s. The following acts are 'grave breaches' of the Protocol if committed wilfully and in violation of the Conventions or the Protocol: '(c) Practices of *apartheid* and other inhuman and degrading practices involving outrages upon personal dignity, based on racial discrimination.' Having regard to the definition of self-determination conflicts contained in Article 1 (4) of the Protocol, such a 'grave breach' was an inevitable addition to the list. The precise nexus between armed conflicts and practices of *apartheid* is not clear, but the confusion between the 'cause' for which the conflict is being waged and the conduct in the conflict is clear.

Two proposals in relation to the repression of 'grave breaches' were rejected by the Conference, because the necessary affirmative majority vote of two-thirds could not be secured. The first was a formula on the defence of superior orders which had appeared in the I.C.R.C. and Government Experts' draft placed before the Conference in 1974.[36] This means that each State will apply its own understanding of the customary international law on the subject of superior orders as it emerged from the Charter and Judgment of the Nuremberg I.M.T. in 1945,[37] and from the varying decisions of the national war crimes trials after the Second World War. The second failure was to find a formula for the mandatory extradition of persons accused of 'grave breaches' in cases where the Detaining Power declined, or was unable, to bring the accused to trial. The wide variation in State legislation governing extradition and the political overtones of many allegations of war criminality precluded an acceptable text. The attempt to use the formulae in 'hijacking' conventions was rejected.[38] Certain States are precluded by their Constitutions from extraditing a national for any crime, e.g. Belgium and the German Federal Republic. All that remained of the proposal was a hortatory provision, in Article 88 (2): When circumstances permit . . . the High Contracting Parties shall co-operate in the matter of extradition. They shall give due consideration to the request of the State in whose territory the alleged offence has occurred. However, two additional requirements found a place in Protocol 1 which are not without relevance to the occasions when superior orders might be pleaded with success to a charge of 'grave breaches'. Under the Conventions of 1949 and Protocol 1 there is a duty upon States to disseminate those instruments, in time of peace, as widely as possible, and 'to include the study thereof by the civilian population so that these instruments may become known to the armed forces and to the civilian population'. (Article 83 of Protocol 1.) Bearing in mind that the members of a N.L.M. must come from within the population of a State, the implementation of this provision in time of peace might be a salutary undertaking. Such instruction reduces the credibility of the standard defence of a person accused of war criminality who claims that he did not know that what he was ordered to do was unlawful, or that, because he received such an order, it was his legal duty to obey it or suffer punishment for disobedience.

A further provision has also become relevant in this context. Article 82 of the Protocol, which had no counterpart in the Conventions, stipulates that:

> The High Contracting Parties at all times, and the Parties to the conflict in time of armed conflict, shall ensure that legal advisers are available, when necessary, to advise military commanders at the appropriate level on the application of the Conventions and this Protocol and on the appropriate instruction to be given to the armed forces on this subject.

The use of the phrase 'Parties to the conflict' makes it applicable to N.L.M.s. There can be little doubt but that the making and deposit of a declaration of intent under article 96 (3) will place N.L.M.s under heavy legal obligations which in many cases they will find difficult to meet. Moreover the compliance with these obligations will no less assuredly reduce the chances of the N.L.M. obtaining a military success, the necessary route for the transition from a N.L.M. to a government.

d: Conclusions:

The intrusion of N.L.M.s into the modern Humanitarian Law governing international armed conflicts is in fundamental contradiction to the principle of non-discrimination which informs that law and the regimes of human rights. Above all, the application of the Humanitarian Law of Armed Conflicts is in no way dependent upon the 'just' or 'unjust' nature of the 'cause' for which the conflict is being waged by the Parties.[39] The 'cause' for which N.L.M.s operate, is, upon analysis, based upon race or alienage. Apart from its vagueness that principle or right of self-determination is discriminatory. The legal proposition that rebellion within a State was not the concern of international law has now become obsolete. If the Declaration of Principles on International Law of 1970 is to be considered as law, there is now a right to rebel for certain specified 'causes', racial in nature. Furthermore, such a 'right' in international law places a correlative 'duty' upon the State concerned not to resist the exercise of such right of self-determination by force. That is in effect a modification of Articles 2 (4) and 51 of the U.N. Charter, the paramount instrument of international law. It adds to the prohibition of the right to use force or the threat of it, contained in the former, and diminishes the right, inherent in all States, of self-defence under the latter. If such be the effect of the Declaration on Principles of 1970, then the penultimate clause thereof:

Nothing in this Declaration shall be construed as prejudicing in any manner the provisions of the Charter or the rights of peoples under the Charter, taking into account the elaboration of these rights in this Declaration.[40]

makes the Declaration repugnant within itself and contradictory. The inherent ambiguity and contradiction in this clause indicates the failure of its redactors to mask the fact that the U.N. Charter was being amended in a manner that had no vestige of legality. One does not remove the distinction between the interpretation and the amendment of a basic legal instrument by designating the latter with the title of the former.

The long story of evils done in the name of the 'just war' doctrine whereby the 'cause', the *jus ad bellum*, controlled the application of the *jus in bello* for the benefit of one belligerent and the detriment of the other,[41] is not something which the international community can afford to resurrect. In terms of the humanitarian protection afforded to members of N.L.M.s engaged in armed conflict, that afforded by Protocol 2 and Article 3 common to the conventions of 1949 was adequate, but it was not compatible with military success. The need to be placed on a level with States on the assumption that N.L.M. struggles were international armed conflicts to which the Conventions of 1949 and Protocol 1 were applicable, was not a humanitarian requirement, but political and military.

The elevation of N.L.M.s into the ambit of Protocol 1 was a political *coup* for those movements. The damage to Humanitarian Law, the benefit of which they have claimed, is apparent because discrimination has been imported into it. It does violence to the facts, including the political and military facts, of the situation. Even with the palliatives in Protocol 1, Article 96 (3), the declaration of intent made during the conflict, and the interpretative statements made by certain states before the signing of the Final Act of the Conference as to the minimum level of intensity of the conflict being determined by reference to the scope provision (Article 1) of Protocol 2, the international community is likely to be confronted with entities bound by a body of humanitarian law that they are unable to apply, even if they had the will to do so. The net effect of the 'political *coup*' obtained by the adoption of the N.L.M. insertion, Article 1 (4) of Protocol 1, is to weaken the delicate network of humanitarian rules established for the conduct of international armed conflicts and at the same time to diminish confidence in Protocol 2 governing internal disputes. That latter instrument is but a pale ghost of the original version that was put before the Conference in 1974. It has shrunk from 42 Articles to 28, and many of the Articles that remain have lost much of their strength. That is a loss because the post-1945 experience of internal conflicts has showed that conduct in such conflicts stands particularly in need of humanitarian legal restraints. This deficiency in restraints is aggravated by the lack of an international monitoring system.

What has been hoped for by a number of States concerned to reaffirm and to widen the Humanitarian Law of Armed Conflicts is that N.L.M.s will prove to be but ephemeral and transitory phenomena. In the present climate of international affairs such a hope may well prove unrealistic.

It was said by the late Sir Hersch Lauterpacht that 'if international law is, in some ways, the vanishing point of law, the law of war is, perhaps, even more conspicuously, at the vanishing point of international law.'[42] It cannot be said that the 'N.L.M. insertion' in Protocol 1 has done much to detract from the truth of that observation. If there be a fundamental human right of 'self-determination of peoples', as the two U.N. Covenants on Human Rights of 1966 have established, then it would seem that, in juridical terms, struggles for self-determination, limited to those against racist and alien regimes, should have found a place in Protocol 2, the sole instrument governing internal conflicts and, as such, dealing with a hostile relationship between the governed and the government.

A breach has been made in the doctrine, first formulated over 300 years ago by Grotius in his fundamentally humanitarian approach to the law of war: 'the question of the justice or injustice of the war is irrelevant for the purpose of observing the rules of warfare as between the belligerents.'[43] The Humanitarian Law of Armed Conflicts established by the Geneva Conventions of 1949 rejected discrimination and the relevance of the 'cause' for which conflicts were waged. Between the essential nature of Humanitarian Law and discrimination there is, and always will be, a fundamental antithesis. The Protocols additional to the Conventions were likewise framed on the basis of the rejection of discrimination.[44] The N.L.M. insertion placed in the controlling scope provision, (Article 1 (4)), of Protocol 1 seeks to accommodate the principle of discrimination in a regime of rules in which it has no place and to which it is opposed. Such was a doubtful service to the advancement of the Rule of the Humanitarian Law of Armed Conflict, a necessarily fragile part of the international legal order. It is possible that this alien insertion in the new Law of War can be limited and contained. Governments will have to act in good faith in applying such law in N.L.M. armed conflicts even if there be no reciprocal response. By such means the political advantage obtained at a law-making conference need not become a legal disaster. Political, military, and juridical realities of our time can give no place to a revived 'just war' doctrine or to a renewed merger of *jus ad bellum* with *jus in bello*.

NOTES

1. M. E. Keen, *The Laws of War in the Late Middle Ages* (London, 1965), pp. 15–22.
2. Ibid., pp. 137–55, 184–5.
3. A. Nussbaum, *A Concise History of the Law of Nations* (revised edn., New York, 1958), p. 72.

4. Keen, op. cit., pp. 73–4.
5. H. Grotius, *De Jure belli ac Pacis* (1625), Book III, chap. IV, para. 14.
6. Nussbaum, op. cit., pp. 224–30.
7. E. W. Hall, *A Treatise on International Law* (8th Edn., London, 1924), p. 82.
8. Article 12 (1).
9. L. Oppenheim, *International Law*, Vol. II: *Disputes, War and Neutrality* (London, 1955), 7th edn. by H. Lauterpacht pp. 181–97.
10. General Assembly Resolution 3314 (XXIX), December 1974.
11. Oppenheim, op. cit., pp. 217–44.
12. C. W. Jenks, 'Lauterpacht – The Scholar and Prophet', *The British Year Book of International Law*, XXXVI (1960), p. 83.
13. *U.N. Treaty Series*, 75 (1950), 1, Nos. 970–3.
14. As at 30 June 1977; *International Review of the Red Cross*, July 1977, No. 196, p. 393 (English version).
15. I. Brownlie (ed.) *Basic Documents in International Law* 2nd edn. (Oxford, 1972), at pp. 146, 163, and 211.
16. Article 1 of the Regulations annexed to Hague Convention No. IV of 1907. *U.N. Treaty Series*, op. cit., p. 138; Article 4 A (2) of the Geneva (P.O.W.) Convention, 1949.
17. Article 2, Hague Regulations, 1907; Article 4 A (6), Geneva (P.O.W.) Convention, 1949.
18. *Draft Rules for the Limitation of the Dangers incurred by the Civilian Population in Time of War*, I.C.R.C., Geneva, Sept. 1956.
19. *Draft Additional Protocols to the Geneva Conventions of August 12, 1949, Commentary*, Doc. CCDH/3, I.C.R.C., Geneva, Oct. 1973.
20. *International Review of the Red Cross*, op. cit., pp. 338–9.
21. Conference Doc. CCDH/400.
22. Protocol 1, Articles 92 and 95; Protocol 2, Articles 20 and 23.
23. 14 December 1960; Brownlie, op. cit., p. 189.
24. General Assembly Resolution 2625 (XXV); Brownlie, op. cit., pp. 38–9.
25. Protocol 2, Article 1 (1).
26. Adopted without vote.
27. H. Lauterpacht, *International Law; Collected Papers*, vol. 2 (Cambridge, 1975), p. 37.
28. Protocol 1, Articles 9 (1), 69 (1), 70 and 75 (4).
29. See note 5, *supra*.
30. Protocol 1, Articles 92 and 94.
31. e.g. the reservations of the Soviet States to Articles 10/10/10/11, common to the four Geneva Conventions, 1949; *U.N. Treaty Series*, op. cit., pp. 458–60.
32. Protocol 1, Articles 51 (6), 52 (1), 53 (c), 54 (4), 55 (2) and 56 (4).
33. Articles 48/50/129/146 common to the four Geneva Conventions, 1949; *U.N. Treaty Series*, op. cit., pp. 62, 116, 236, and 386.
34. (1850), c. 169. 64 Stat. 108.
35. Protocol 1, Articles 1 (6) and 52 (1).

36. I.C.R.C. Commentary, op. cit., p. 97. Draft Article 77 was not acceptable to the Conference and attempts to agree a substitute text were unsuccessful.

37. The Charter to the London Agreement, 1845, Article 8; I.M.T. *Judgment* (Nuremberg), H.M.S.O. Cmd. (6964), p. 42.

38. e.g. Article 8 of the Hague Convention on the Unlawful Seizure of Aircraft, 1970, and Article 8 of the Montreal Convention on the Suppression of Unlawful Acts against the Safety of Civil Aviation, 1971.

39. This is emphasized in the penultimate preambular para. to Protocol 1 : '*Reaffirming* that the provisions of the Geneva Conventions . . . 1949, and of this Protocol must be fully applied in all circumstances to all persons who are protected by these instruments without any adverse distinction based on the nature or origin of the armed conflict or on the causes espoused by or attributed to the Parties to the conflict.'

40. Brownlie, op. cit., p. 40.

41. Nussbaum, op. cit., p. 72.

42. H. Lauterpacht, 'The Revision of the Law of War', *The British Year Book of International Law*, vol. xxix (1952), pp. 381–2.

43. See note 5, *supra.*

44. See note 38, *supra.*

SELECT READING LIST

1. General

BAILEY, S. D., *Prohibitions and Restraints in War*, Oxford, 1972.
BROWNLIE, I., *International Law and the Use of Force by States*, Oxford, 1963.
CASTRÉN, E., *The Present Law of War and Neutrality*, Helsinki, 1954.
HALL, W., *Treatise on International Law*, 8th edn., ed. A. Pearce Higgins, London, 1924.
KALSHOVEN, F., *The Law of Warfare: a Summary of Recent History and Trends*, Leyden, 1973.
KOTSCH, L., *The Concept of War in Contemporary History and International Law*, Geneva, 1956.
LAUTERPACHT, H., *International Law and Human Rights*, London, 1950.
OPPENHEIM, L., *International Law*, vol. II: *Disputes, War and Neutrality*, 7th edn., ed. H. Lauterpacht, London, 1955.
SCHWARZENBERGER, G., *A Manual of International Law*, London, 1947.
STONE, J., *Legal Controls of International Conflict*, London, 1959.

2. Restraints on War by Land before 1945

BOISSIER, P., *Histoire du Comité Internationale de la Croix Rouge*, vol. 1: *De Solférino à Tsoushima*, Paris, 1963.
FALK, R., and others, *Crimes of War*, New York, 1971.
GREENSPAN, M., *The Modern Law of Land Warfare*, Berkeley, 1959.
HOLLAND, T. E., *Letters to 'The Times' Upon War and Neutrality*, London 1909, 1914, 1921.
ROLIN, A., *Le Droit moderne de la guerre*, Brussels, 1921.
SPAIGHT, J. M., *War Rights on Land*, London, 1911.
VEALE, F. J. P., *Advance to Barbarism: the Development of Total Warfare from Sarajevo to Hiroshima*, London, 1948.
WESTLAKE, J., *International Law*, vol. 2: *War*, 2nd edn., Cambridge, 1913.

3. Restraints on War at Sea before 1945.

ARNOLD FOSTER, W., *The New Freedom of the Seas*, London, 1942.
MARCUS, G., *A Naval History of England*, 2 vols., London 1961, 1971.
MARDER, A. J., *The Anatomy of British Sea Power: a History of British Naval Policy in the Pre-Dreadnought Era 1880–1905*, London, 1964. *From the Dreadnought to Scapa Flow: the Royal Navy in the Fisher Era, 1904–1915*, 5 vols., London, 1961–70.
PIGGOTT, F. T., *The Declaration of Paris, 1856*, London, 1919.
RICHMOND, H., *Statesmen and Sea Power*, Oxford, 1946.
ROSKILL, S. W., *Naval Policy between the Wars*, 2 vols., London, 1968, 1976.

SAVAGE, C., *Policy of the United States towards Maritime Commerce in War*, 2 vols., Washington, 1934, reprinted N.Y., 1969.
See also the works of Hall, Oppenheim, and Schwarzenberger cited in section (1) above.

4. Restraints on War in the Air before 1945.

BIALER, U., 'Some Aspects of the Fear of Bombardment from the Air and the Making of British Defence and Foreign Policy, 1932–39', University of London Ph.D. thesis, 1974.
CHAPUT, R. A., *Disarmament in British Foreign Policy*, London, 1935.
GIBBS, N. H., *Grand Strategy*, vol. 1 (U.K. Official Histories of the Second World War, Military Series, ed. J. R. M. Butler), London, 1976.
GROVES, P. A. C., *Behind the Smoke Screen*, London, 1934.
HYDE, H. MONTGOMERY, *British Air Policy between the Wars 1918-1939*, London, 1976.
JONES, H. A., *The War in the Air*, vol. VI. Oxford, 1922.
POWERS, B., *Strategy without Slide-rule: British Air Strategy 1914–1939*, London, 1976.
QUESTER, G. H., *Deterrence before Hiroshima. The Air Power Background of Modern Strategy*, New York, 1928.
ROYSE, M. W., *Aerial Bombardment and the International Regulation of Warfare*, New York, 1928.
SAUNDBY, R., *Air Bombardment*, London, 1961.
WEBSTER, C., and FRANKLAND, A. N., *The Strategic Air Offensive against Germany*, vols. 1 and IV (U.K. Official Histories of the Second World War, Military Series), London, 1961.

5. Limited War in the Nuclear Age: 'Conventional' Conflicts

BRODIE, B., *Strategy in the Missile Age*, Princeton, 1959.
HALPERIN, M. H., *Limited War: an Essay on the Development of the Theory*, Center for International Affairs, Harvard University, 1962.
KISSINGER, H. A., *Nuclear Weapons and Foreign Policy*, New York, 1957.
KNORR, K., *On the Uses of Military Power in the Nuclear Age*, Princeton, 1966.
LIDDELL-HART, B. H., *Deterrence or Defence*, London, 1960.
McCLINTOCK, R., *The Meaning of Limited War*, Boston, 1967.
OSGOOD, R. E., *Limited War: the Challenge to American Strategy*, Chicago, 1957.
SCHELLING, T. C., *The Strategy of Conflict*, Cambridge, Mass., 1960.
SNYDER, G. H., *Deterrence and Defence: Towards a Theory of National Security*, Princeton, 1961.

6. Limited Nuclear War

DAVIS, L. E., *Limited Nuclear Options: Deterrence and the New American Doctrine*, Adelphi Paper No. 121, International Institute for Strategic Studies, London, 1976.

DOUGLASS, J. D., *The Soviet Theater Nuclear Offensive*, Washington, D.C., 1976.
KNORR, K. and READ, T., *Limited Strategic War*, London and New York, 1962.
MARTIN, L., 'Flexibility in Tactical Nuclear Response', in Holst, J. and Nehrlich, U., *Beyond Nuclear Deterrence*, New York, 1977.
SCHLESINGER, J., *The Theater Nuclear Force Posture in Europe: a Report to Congress, 1 April 1975*, Washington, D.C.. 1975.

7. Limited Conflict at Sea since 1945.

ALLISON, G. T., *Essence of Decision: Explaining the Cuban Missile Crisis*, New York, 1971.
BROCK, J. R., 'Hot pursuit and the right of pursuit' in *JAG Journal of the U.S. Navy*, vol. XVIII, 1960.
BROWN, E. D., *Arms Control in Hydrospace: Legal Aspects*, Woodrow Wilson Center for International Scholars, Washington, D.C., 1971.
CABLE, J., *Gunboat Diplomacy*, London, 1971.
CARLISLE, G. E., 'The interrelationship of international law and U.S.-naval operations in south-east Asia', in *JAG Journal of the US Navy*, vol. XXII, 1967.
CLARK, J. J. C. and BARNES, D. H. B., *Sea Power and its Meaning*, London, 1966.
COLVIN, R. D., 'The aftermath of Elath' in *Proceedings of the U.S. Naval Institute*, vol. XCV, June 1969.
HARLOW, B., 'Legal use of force short of war' in *Proceedings of the U.S. Naval Institute*, vol. XCII, 1966.
HILL, J. R., 'Maritime forces in confrontation', *Brassey's Annual*, London, 1972.
LAWRENCE, K. D., 'Military-legal considerations in the extension of the territorial seas', *Military Law Review*, vol. XXIX, 1965.
LUCEY, M. N., 'Resources of the Sea', *Brassey's Annual*, London, 1972.
MARTIN, L. W., *The Sea in Modern Strategy*, London 1968.
O'CONNELL, D. P., 'International Law and contemporary naval operations', *British Year Book of International Law*, vol. XLIV, 1970.
O'CONNELL, D. P., 'The Legality of naval cruise missiles', *American Journal of International Law*, vol. 66, 1972.
—— *The Influence of Law on Sea Power*, Manchester, 1974.

8. Wars of National Liberation and War Criminality

DRAPER, G. I. A. D., *The Red Cross Conventions*, London, 1958.
—— 'The Geneva Conventions', *Hague Recueil des Cours*, vol. 1, Leyden, 1965.
KEEN, M., *The Laws of War in the late Middle Ages*, London, 1965.

KOSSOY, E., *Living with Guerrilla : Guerrilla as a Legal Problem and a Political Fact*, Geneva, 1976.

PICTET, J. (ed.), *Commentaries on the Geneva Conventions of 1949*, 4 vols., Geneva, 1952–60.

See also the works by Lauterpacht, Oppenheim, and Stone cited in section (1) above.

INDEX